The LAURA INGALLS WILDER *Companion*

The LAURA INGALLS WILDER Companion

A Chapter-by-Chapter Guide

ANNETTE WHIPPLE

Published by Chicago Review Press Incorporated
814 North Franklin Street
Chicago, Illinois 60610
ISBN 978-1-64160-166-5

Library of Congress Cataloging-in-Publication Data
Names: Whipple, Annette, author.
Title: The Laura Ingalls Wilder companion : a chapter-by-chapter guide / Annette Whipple.
Description: Chicago : Chicago Review Press, [2020] | Audience: Ages 9 to 12 | Audience: Grades 4-6 | Summary: "The Laura Ingalls Wilder Companion helps eager readers experience and discover Wilder's books like never before. Author Annette Whipple encourages children to engage in pioneer activities while thinking deeper about the stories and real-life circumstances of the Ingalls and Wilder families as portrayed in the nine Little House books. This valuable companion provides brief introductions to each Little House book, chapter-by-chapter story guides, and additional information related to each of the books' content and history. "Fact or Fiction" sidebars tell the surprising truth about Laura Ingalls Wilder's writing, while 75 activities, crafts, and recipes encourage kids to "Live Like Laura" using easy-to-find supplies. Thoughtful questions help the reader develop appreciation and understanding for stories. Every aspiring adventurer will enjoy this walk alongside Laura from the big woods to the golden years"— Provided by publisher.
Identifiers: LCCN 2020005800 (print) | LCCN 2020005801 (ebook) | ISBN 9781641601665 (trade paperback) | ISBN 9781641601672 (pdf) | ISBN 9781641601689 (mobi) | ISBN 9781641601696 (epub)
Subjects: LCSH: Wilder, Laura Ingalls, 1867-1957—Criticism and interpretation—Juvenile literature. | Wilder, Laura Ingalls, 1867-1957—Appreciation—Juvenile literature. | Frontier and pioneer life in literature—Juvenile literature. | Frontier and pioneer life—Problems, exercises, etc.
Classification: LCC PS3545.I342 Z967 2020 (print) | LCC PS3545.I342 (ebook) | DDC 813/.52 [B]—dc23
LC record available at https://lccn.loc.gov/2020005800
LC ebook record available at https://lccn.loc.gov/2020005801

Cover design: Natalya Balnova
Interior design: Jonathan Hahn
Interior illustrations: Jim Spence
Map design: Chris Erichsen

Printed in the United States of America
5 4 3 2 1

For Meghan, Evan, and Esther

CONTENTS

A NOTE FOR THE READER

Dear Reader,

I remember the Little House books from my elementary school's library stacks, when Mrs. Rhinehart shelved them in the back of the library. I visited those shelves again and again. Laura Ingalls Wilder's stories stayed with me throughout my life; I returned to the books as an adult and loved the stories even more. Then I shared them with my children.

The books made my children ask questions. We talked about the complicated pioneer history. Together we made johnnycakes and danced to fiddle music. I even sewed an apron and bonnet for my oldest daughter's sixth birthday.

I wrote this companion guide to help you live like Laura too. As you read a Little House book (or the whole series), use this guide to help you understand Laura's world. You can even get a taste of pioneer life with activities and recipes!

Think of *The Laura Ingalls Wilder Companion* as a visitor's guide, but instead of visiting a city you'll meet the Ingalls family in its pages. You can visit a faraway city without a guide, but you wouldn't want to travel back in time without understanding life long ago. This book will help you enter the world and life of Laura Ingalls Wilder. It will also help you think about history—the Ingalls family history *and* American history.

THE BOOKS

Laura Ingalls Wilder based the Little House books on her childhood. The books are historical fiction, so not *every* word the author wrote is true. But they are based on real people, places, and events.

Wilder included some tough subjects in her books because they portrayed her own experience as a pioneer. She wrote about how white settlers treated the

American Indians—and it was often shameful. But there were good lessons too. Her childhood focused on hard work, independence, and the importance of family. These topics, good and bad, are Wilder's story, but they're also America's story—our history. We need to think about these issues even when they make us uncomfortable.

HOW TO USE THIS BOOK

Part I of *The Laura Ingalls Wilder Companion* is dedicated to Wilder's stories about her (and Almanzo's) childhood as she told them in the Little House books. Read the companion chapter in this book while reading the corresponding Little House book. In these chapters you'll explore history and learn more about the real people and places in the "Dig Deeper" sections. Next, a variety of activities and recipes will help you "Live Like Laura" and Almanzo. And finally, you'll find "House Talk" questions. You might answer these as you read or after you finish a Little House book. They are especially fun to discuss with a friend or family member.

The character of Laura Ingalls grows up in the books just as the author did in real life. You can read about her adult life in Part II, which includes the companion chapter for *The First Four Years* as well as biographical information about the Ingalls family.

Some of the words used in the Little House books aren't familiar to readers today. You'll find hundreds of definitions for these words in "Pioneer Terms." They're listed in alphabetical order at the end of this book.

You might want to learn even more about Laura Ingalls Wilder. So I've included resources about her for you to explore (see page 167).

A FINAL NOTE

Although Laura Ingalls Wilder and her family were some of the first white Americans to live where they did, they weren't famous pioneers. At least, they weren't famous at the time when they were pioneers. Now their names are known around the world because of the Little House books.

Millions of Little House books have been sold globally since *Little House in the Big Woods*, the first in the series, was published in 1932. A popular television show called *Little House on the Prairie* introduced the Ingalls family to even more fans in the 1970s and '80s. Now it's your turn to read about this pioneer family.

And as Ma would say, "All's well that ends well."

Happy trails,

Annette Whipple

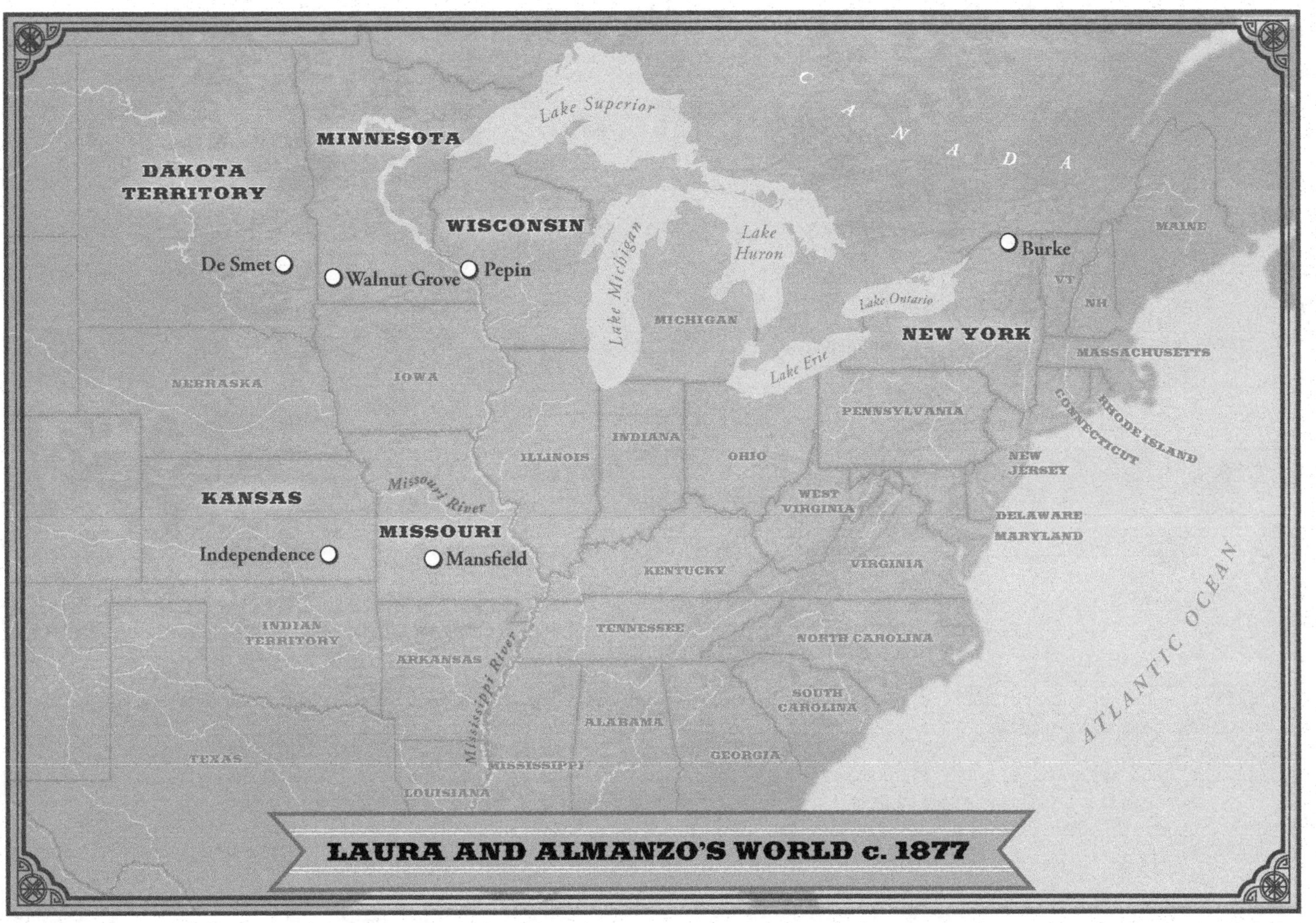
CANADA
Lake Superior
MINNESOTA
DAKOTA TERRITORY
WISCONSIN
De Smet
Walnut Grove
Pepin
Lake Michigan
Lake Huron
MICHIGAN
Lake Ontario
Lake Erie
Burke
NEW YORK
MAINE
VT
NH
MASSACHUSETTS
RHODE ISLAND
CONNECTICUT
NEW JERSEY
DELAWARE
MARYLAND
NEBRASKA
IOWA
PENNSYLVANIA
ILLINOIS
INDIANA
OHIO
WEST VIRGINIA
KANSAS
Missouri River
MISSOURI
Independence
Mansfield
KENTUCKY
VIRGINIA
INDIAN TERRITORY
TENNESSEE
NORTH CAROLINA
ARKANSAS
Mississippi River
SOUTH CAROLINA
ALABAMA
TEXAS
MISSISSIPPI
GEORGIA
LOUISIANA
ATLANTIC OCEAN
LAURA AND ALMANZO'S WORLD c. 1877

PART I

LITTLE LAURA

"Some old-fashioned things like fresh air and sunshine are hard to beat."

—Laura Ingalls Wilder, *Missouri Ruralist*, 1916

This log cabin was built to match the description of the Ingallses' home in *Little House in the Big* Woods. *Courtesy of The Laura Ingalls Wilder Museum, Pepin, Wisconsin*

1

Little House in the Big Woods

PEPIN, WISCONSIN

Pa, Ma, Mary, Laura, and Carrie Ingalls lived in their little log cabin near Pepin, Wisconsin. Life in the Big Woods was full of work. The family spent their days close to home. Each season had its own chores, and the children helped with all the work. They raised or caught their food. And they made everything in their home—even socks and furniture.

Despite all the work, they still had time for fun. Pa fiddled for the family at night, and Ma cut paper dolls for the girls. They celebrated with their grandparents and other family members when they could. Compared to modern families, the Ingallses' life was simple. They were busy, but it was a different kind of busy.

As you read, you'll learn about the family and pioneer living through the eyes of four-year-old Laura in this first Little House book.

Laura Ingalls Wilder called this book *Little Girl in the Big Woods* before it was published. Another title considered was *Trundle-Bed Tales.* It was published in 1932 with the final title of *Little House in the Big Woods.* Wilder didn't know it would be part of a series, but it was the first of nine novels that would make up the Little House series. Each of the Little House books focuses on family life in the late 1800s.

DIG DEEPER

Chapter 1

- *Little House in the Big Woods* takes place in 1871 and 1872, about 150 years ago.
- On the opening page, Laura Ingalls Wilder wrote that there were no houses near the Ingalls family. Though they couldn't see any homes from their cabin,

they did have neighbors. Relatives lived nearby. They could even walk to their houses.

- Salting meat preserved it by keeping germs from growing. It also gave the meat extra flavor.
- Laura Ingalls Wilder was born 7 miles (11 km) northwest of Pepin, Wisconsin, in 1867. Pepin is still a small village today.

BUTCHERING TIME

Most pioneers raised or hunted meat instead of buying it. Pa did too. He raised a hog for meat. He hunted wild animals.

Laura Ingalls Wilder wanted readers to understand all the work needed before eating a meal. This included garden work and preparing meat. Many people dislike reading about butchering time. You might even think Wilder included too many details about it.

Today we often eat meat without thinking about where it came from. We might buy meat from the grocery store, but farmers raise the animals first. When the animals are big enough, they're sold. Butchers or factories prepare the meat. Then it's sent to a grocery store so customers can buy it.

Chapter 2

- Pa's bear excited the whole family. The bear provided the family a lot of meat during the cold winter months. The hog's meat gave them another type of meat to eat during meals.
- The Laura Ingalls Wilder Historic Home and Museum in Mansfield, Missouri, now displays Pa's actual fiddle. The original fiddle case is dated 1850.
- Without medical help, animals—and people—died from rabies. An animal infected with rabies acts strangely and sometimes foams at the mouth. A dog with rabies was often called a "mad dog." Today veterinarians and doctors treat rabies with medication.

Chapter 3

- Pa's gun was a single-shot rifle. It fired only once, and then he reloaded it.
- An emergency could happen at any time, especially with wild animals. Pa stored his gun above the door. He could easily grab it on his way out the door, but it was too high for the children to reach.

Chapter 4

- Prince's behavior worried Aunt Eliza. The dog didn't obey. He seemed naughty, but he protected Aunt Eliza.
- "Children should be seen and not heard" was often said in pioneer times. Parents expected children in the 1800s to be silent unless spoken to by an adult. The Ingalls children understood this as a way of life.

Chapter 5

- The family typically took baths every Saturday. Like many pioneers, they bathed just once a week. Pioneer families with small homes often made a private area by hanging a blanket as a wall. (Bathrooms were not common until later in the 1900s.) Pioneers collected water from a spring, creek, or well during warm months and carried it to their stove to heat. During the winter months, they brought snow inside and melted it on the stove.
- The Sabbath is a day set aside to rest and worship God. The Ingalls family only did strictly necessary work on Sundays. They fed the animals and milked the cows, but other work waited until Monday. Today, many people still rest on the Sabbath, though the way they do it may look very different from how Laura and her family rested.
- Pa's big green book that Ma read from was titled *The Polar and Tropical Worlds* by Georg Hartwig. It had 200 black-and-white illustrations called engravings. It was published in 1871. Owning such a book showed that Charles and Caroline Ingalls thought knowledge was important.
- Laura Ingalls Wilder celebrated her fifth birthday in 1872. She was born on February 7, 1867.
- Laura's five little cakes were probably shortbread or sugar cookies.
- Slavery in the United States ended only four years before Laura was born. However, even after the end of slavery, many white Americans still treated other races, including African Americans, poorly. The song about Uncle Ned used the word "darkey." This term was a common slang word for a black person then. Today the word is considered offensive and should not be used.

Chapter 6

- Like many other pioneers, Pa trapped wild animals. The family ate the meat. Later Pa traded the animal furs in town. Pa brought home fabric and candy for a treat.

Chapter 7

- Ma only wore her delaine dress for special occasions like the sugaring-off dance. It was made from high-quality wool.

Chapter 8

- The original Ingalls cabin in Pepin, Wisconsin, no longer stands. However, Little House fans can visit a recreated cabin built on the land owned by Charles Ingalls. The little house is 22 feet (6.7 m) long and 20 feet (6.1 m) wide on the outside.

Chapter 9

- Mary and Laura loved to go barefoot outdoors. Shoes cost a lot and were uncomfortable, so it made sense to go without them during the warm months, but the girls wore shoes for special occasions like going to town. In the 1870s, cobblers made shoes for most families. Some stores sold premade shoes, but they weren't as common as custom-made ones.
- Lake Pepin is part of the Mississippi River in Wisconsin.

Chapter 10

- Even in the 1800s, scientists had seen the moon through telescopes. American pioneers like the Ingalls family read about the moon in newspapers, magazines, and books.

SUGAR SNOW

All maple trees produce sap, but one kind of maple tree is different than the others. The sugar maple's sap works best for making syrup. The sap flows through the trees in the late winter or early spring. Temperatures must be above freezing during the day and below freezing at night for sap to flow.

Maple farmers still tap trees, just like Laura Ingalls Wilder described in *Little House in the Big Woods*. They put a special spout, called a spile, in a hole drilled into the tree. The clear, sweet sap drips into a bucket or another container. They collect sap every day. Then the maple farmers boil the sap to create different maple products like syrup, candy, and sugar.

It takes about forty gallons of sap (and sometimes more) to make just one gallon of real maple syrup. Other products like maple sugar and maple cakes (often called maple candy today) are made by cooking the sap even longer. You can purchase delicious maple products from maple farms.

Laura Elizabeth Ingalls was born on February 7, 1867, in the family's cabin near Pepin, Wisconsin. *Courtesy of The Laura Ingalls Wilder Museum, Pepin, Wisconsin*

- Today cheesemakers need the same ingredients as Ma did to make cheese: milk and rennet. Animal rennet comes from the lining of a calf, kid (young goat), or lamb's fourth stomach. The rennet changes the milk into solid curds and liquid whey. The whey is squeezed or pressed out. The leftover curds make the cheese.

Chapter 11

- Did the story of Charley's misbehavior remind you of a familiar tale? Aesop's fable "The Boy Who Cried Wolf" was likely well known to the Ingalls family. Charley might have agreed with the moral of the fable. (If you aren't familiar with the story, look up the fable online or find it in a book. Your local library can help you.)
- Yellow jackets are a type of wasp. Bees and wasps are in the same family but are different insects. The sting of a wasp typically hurts more than a bee sting. Wasps are more likely to sting a person repeatedly.

CIVIL WAR SOLDIERS

The Civil War lasted from 1861 to 1865. The United States was divided. The southern states wanted to form their own country and make their own laws. The northern states wanted to stay together as one country. So they fought.

Men ages 18 and older served as soldiers. Boys 17 years old and younger helped as messengers and musicians, including drummers. However, some boys lied about their age so they could fight in the war. Though women weren't supposed to be soldiers, about 400 fought in the Civil War.

The Union soldiers from the north wore blue coats. The southern Confederate soldiers wore gray coats.

Between the two armies, more than 600,000 people lost their lives to battle wounds and disease during the Civil War. The war ended on April 9, 1865, when the South surrendered.

Boys often served in the Civil War as messengers and musicians.
Liljenquist Family collection, Library of Congress

Chapter 12

- Laura learned from her mother. Ma made hats for the entire family, so Laura made a small hat for her doll. As Laura grew up, she had the skills she needed to make full-size hats for herself and her own family.
- As you read, did you wonder what wonderful machine prepared the wheat so quickly? Pa called it a separator. It's also known as a thresher. It separates the edible grain (like oats, wheat, or barley) from the stalks they grow on. Years later, the combine harvester became popular. The combine helped farmers even more by harvesting grain *and* threshing it.
- Wheat is a type of grass grown for its kernels. Flour is the most popular wheat product people use. Pasta, cereal, and bread are made from flour.

Chapter 13

- Logs work surprisingly well as natural insulators in homes made from them. The areas between the logs let in cold air, however, so they must be chinked—or filled in—with a mud paste. The mud keeps the cold air and critters outside.
- Pa went deer hunting after supper because white-tailed deer are crepuscular. Crepuscular animals are most active at dawn and dusk.

LIVE LIKE LAURA

Homemade Butter

Mary sometimes helped Ma use the butter churn. Laura was too little to use the churn and dasher, but even small kids can make butter using a jar. Friends can help if you get too tired shaking the jar.

What You Need

- heavy cream (or whipping cream)
- salt (optional)

What to Do

Fill a clean jar about halfway with cream. Add a pinch of salt for flavor. Tightly cap the jar. Shake the jar until a ball of hard butter forms. It might take about half an hour. (The liquid—buttermilk—and solid cream separate. This is to be expected.) Keep shaking! When the butter is even more solid, drain the liquid. Squeeze the butter ball in your hand to remove even more buttermilk. Then, rinse the butter ball in cold water.

Try the butter on crackers, biscuits, or bread (see pages 86, 90, and 143 respectively for recipes).. This is real butter—you can even bake with it. Store leftovers in the refrigerator; they'll keep for seven to ten days.

Paper Dolls

Ma made paper dolls for Mary and Laura using stiff paper. Create your own homemade paper dolls like the ones Mary and Laura played with using scraps of pretty paper and fabric.

What You Need

- stiff paper or cardstock
- pencil or pen
- scissors
- colored scrap paper from newspapers, magazines, or wrapping paper
- fabric scraps
- lace or ribbon
- tape or glue (optional)

What to Do

1. Draw a body for a paper doll on the stiff paper.
2. Cut out the paper doll.
3. Draw a face on it.
4. Use scrap fabric, colored paper, or even magazine pages to create clothes and hats for your paper doll. Start by drawing out their shapes on the colorful papers and fabrics.

5. As you draw the outlines of the accessories, add the outline of a tab to each one.
6. Cut around the outlines you made, including the tabs. Add ribbon and scrap fabric to embellish the accessories.

7. Place the accessories on the doll, then fold the tabs behind the paper doll's body to secure the accessories in place. Use tape or glue if needed.
8. Make additional paper dolls for fun.

Vinegar Pie

Ma made vinegar pie for special occasions like Christmas. This pie is easy to make and uses ingredients most pioneers had.

Don't let the name of the pie fool you—it's sweet. The vinegar enhances the flavor of the pie, much like vanilla is added to cookies or cakes today.

What You Need

- pie crust, prepared
- 1 cup (240 mL) brown sugar
- ¼ cup (60 mL) all-purpose flour
- ¼ teaspoon (1 mL) cinnamon
- ⅛ teaspoon (0.5 mL) nutmeg
- 1 cup (240 mL) water
- 2 eggs, at room temperature
- ¼ cup (60 mL) butter, melted
- 1 tablespoon (15 mL) apple cider vinegar

What to Do

1. Preheat oven to 400°F (200°C).
2. Line the bottom of a pie pan with the pie crust. Crimp the edges.
3. In a medium-sized bowl combine sugar, flour, cinnamon, and nutmeg. Mix well.
4. Stir in the water, eggs, butter, and vinegar. Mix well.
5. Pour the filling into the pie crust and bake for 35 to 40 minutes.
6. Serve at room temperature.

Snow Pictures

The cousins played outside together at Christmas time. Alice, Ella, Peter, Mary, and Laura made pictures of themselves in the snow. You can make your own snow pictures if you have deep enough snow. Be careful: if the snow isn't deep, you might get hurt.

In deep snow, climb onto a stump, big rock, or a stair step. Hold your arms out wide and fall forward. Get up very carefully so your snow picture isn't disturbed. Have fun trying different arm and leg positions. Try a backward snow picture too.

Pancake People

Ma made a pancake man for each of the children on Christmas Day. Make your own pancake people like Ma cooked for a special treat.

What You Need

- pancake batter
- griddle
- spoon
- chocolate chips
- butter, maple syrup, and brown sugar (optional)

What to Do

1. Make pancake batter and follow the recipe's instructions to prepare the griddle.
2. Using a spoon, place a spoonful of batter on the griddle for the head.
3. Working quickly, add the arms, body, and legs. Get more batter as needed.
4. When the edges are dry and bubbly, flip the pancake person over, using a spatula. You may want to cook the people a little longer than usual so they do not break when flipping.
5. After flipping, add chocolate chips for eyes, for fun.
6. When the underside is brown and cooked, place the pancake person on a plate.
7. Enjoy with butter and maple syrup or brown sugar.

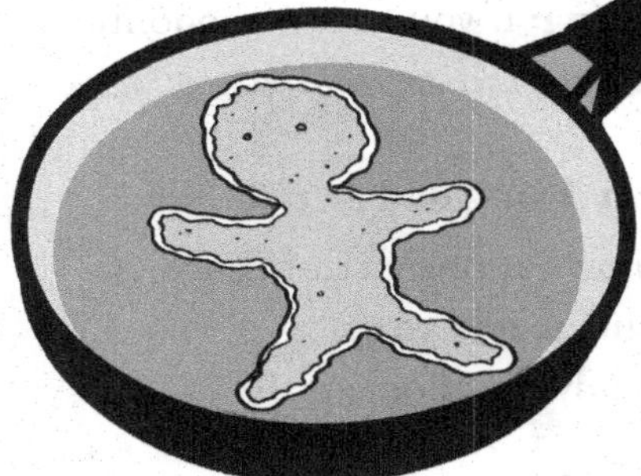

The Quiet Challenge

When Laura became frustrated with a quiet Sunday, Pa shared a story of how much harder it was for his father on Sundays. Can you be as quiet and as still as Pa's father?

Go to a church service or another adult-oriented meeting with your family and see if you can sit very still. Can you go without talking, looking out windows, or fidgeting during the entire service? To be like Grandpa, keep your legs from swinging. Be sure to tell your parents your plan before the service begins. Afterward, discuss the experience.

Visit a Maple Farm

Pa helped Grandpa collect sap from maple trees to turn into syrup and candy.

Contact a maple farm to learn all about collecting sap and making syrup. Arrange a visit when they are actively making syrup. For sap to flow, nighttime temperatures need to be below freezing while daytime temperatures are above freezing. This is typically late winter or early spring.

If visiting isn't possible in your area or you are reading this in the summer, watch an online video about maple syrup production.

Snow Maple Candy

Grandma and Grandpa Ingalls hosted a dance at their home. They wanted to celebrate the sugar snow. Laura and her family arrived early to help. The men worked to gather and boil sap. The women made food for the evening feast.

You don't need a party to make your own snow maple candy, but you will need real maple syrup and snow (or a snow substitute).

Warning: if you have orthodontic work such as braces, avoid eating this candy. *Adult supervision required.*

What You Need

- snow (or finely crushed ice)
- pure maple syrup
- candy thermometer

What to Do

1. Gather fresh snow in a shallow bowl or pie pan. Pack it into the bowl. Set the snow pan outside or in the freezer.

2. Place a small amount (about ½ cup or 120 mL) of maple syrup in a sauce pan.
3. Have an adult cook the syrup over medium-high heat and bring it to a boil.
4. The adult should continue boiling the maple syrup until it reaches 235°F (115°C). Then drizzle the thickened maple liquid over the snow.
5. Allow to cool in the snow for about a minute. Then break off a piece of maple snow candy to enjoy while it's cold.

Dance a Jig

Grandma and Uncle George got so excited about their jig that Grandma nearly forgot about the maple sap cooking on the stove.

Look for videos of jigs online. See how they keep their feet moving? Turn up the music and see if you can keep your feet jigging too!

Clove-Apple

Grandma kept a clove-apple beside her sewing basket. It made the house smell good. Create a sweet-smelling clove apple as a gift or a decoration.

Cloves preserve the apple while providing a spicy, fragrant scent. They must be placed near one another, but not touching, to prevent the clove-apple from going bad quickly. You can even create clove designs, but the apple will begin decomposing sooner if the cloves are not placed close together.

What You Need

- apple (with a stem and no bruises or blemishes)
- whole cloves (a large quantity)
- ribbon, twine, or yarn

What to Do

1. Push the stem of one clove into the apple skin.
2. Add more cloves until the cloves cover the apple.
3. Tie the yarn to the stem of the apple when finished.
4. Hang the clove-apple in a pantry, closet, or other dark, dry place to enjoy its scent.

Rag Curls

After their baths, Ma used rags to tie up Mary and Laura's hair. Their hair was curly the next day.

Victorian rag curls are beautiful. Use long fabric strips to make your own today. These directions show one way to make rag curls on another person. To do it on yourself, you may need a hair clip to hold the strip of cloth in place.

What You Need

- spray water bottle (optional)
- hair mousse or gel (optional)
- comb or brush
- 5–10 strips of cloth, 3–4 inches (8–10 cm) wide and twice as long as the length of the hair
- hair ties, pins, or clips (optional)

What to Do

1. Comb damp hair thoroughly to remove knots. If beginning with dry hair, spritz hair with a water bottle until damp. Do not over wet it. If using hair mousse or gel, put it in the hair at this time.
2. Divide all hair into 5 to 10 sections. You can keep each section separate with a hair tie or hair clip or just begin with one section of hair.
3. Begin with a front section. Comb this section of hair. Hold the fabric strip parallel to the hair and have the person getting their hair curled hold the end of the fabric on top of their head to keep it in place. If you're curling your own hair, use a hair clip to secure the fabric strip to the top of your head.
4. Keep the hair flat and wrap the hair around the fabric strip. Wrap the hair going down the fabric. Avoid pulling the hair tight to get thicker curls.
5. Continue wrapping the fabric around the section of hair until you reach the hair tips. Cover the hair tips with the

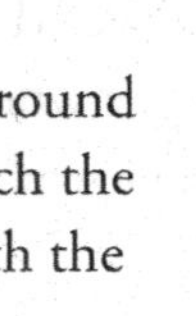

fabric strip, then wrap the fabric going around the hair moving "up" the section of hair toward the scalp.
6. Take the two ends of the fabric and tie securely near the scalp.
7. Repeat the process for the other sections of hair. Try to wrap the curls for each section of hair in the same direction.
8. Allow the rag curls to dry completely. The longer you can leave the rags in the hair, the better. Sleep on them to allow enough drying time.
9. The next day untie the curls and remove fabric strips.
10. Split each curl into two or more curls.
11. (Optional) Trying styling the curled hair in different ways.

Stump Jump

The children liked playing in Uncle Henry and Aunt Polly's yard because it had many tree stumps.

Visit a wooded area with several downed trees. Create your own game by climbing on the logs, stumps, or big rocks to stay off the ground. If no woods are available, create an obstacle course that challenges you to stay off the ground using a playset or even small towels and washcloths.

Nut Taste Test

Laura, Mary, and Ma gathered walnuts, hickory nuts, and hazelnuts and placed them in the sun to dry before removing their outer shells. They stored the nuts in the attic for the winter.

Try a variety of nuts to learn which is your favorite. Gather walnuts, hickory nuts, and hazelnuts or purchase a bag of mixed nuts from a store. If buying nuts, buy them with shells for more fun. If you gather them from outdoors, dry them prior to eating. Use a nutcracker or hammer to open each shell. (Be careful! Use safety googles to protect your eyes from flying shells if using a hammer.) Next, try each type of nut. Which do you like best?

Warning: Avoid this activity if allergic to nuts.

Johnnycakes

Johnnycakes are made with cornmeal, so they taste like corn bread. They can be baked or fried on a griddle like pancakes. Enjoy them with butter or maple syrup.

Adult supervision required.

What You Need

- 1 cup (240 mL) cornmeal
- 1 teaspoon (5 mL) granulated sugar
- ½ teaspoon (2.5 mL) salt
- 1¼ cup (300 mL) boiling water
- 3 tablespoons (45 mL) oil or shortening (use more if needed)

What to Do

Note: Use caution with this recipe. The oil gets very hot and splatters.

1. Mix the cornmeal, sugar, and salt together in a bowl.
2. Have an adult warm a griddle or frying pan over medium heat. It is warm enough when sprinkled water "dances" across the heated surface. (Use a griddle or frying pan made of cast iron or with a nonstick coating. Avoid using an aluminum pan because the johnnycakes will stick to it.)
3. Slowly add the boiling water to the cornmeal mixture. Stir until just combined. Do not overmix.
4. Place 1 tablespoon (15 mL) of oil or shortening on the warm griddle.
5. Place one large spoonful of batter on the oiled griddle.
6. After the edges turn golden brown, wait another 30 seconds and then flip the johnnycake with a wide spatula.
7. Gently flatten the center of the johnnycake with the back of the spatula. The second side does not take as long as the first to cook. When the bottom turns golden brown, remove the cooked johnnycake and begin again. Add more oil or shortening to the griddle if the cakes begin to stick.
8. Serve warm with butter, molasses, or maple syrup.

HOUSE TALK

- Think about the Big Woods of Wisconsin as described in the book. What would you like about living there? What would you dislike?
- As pioneers, the Ingallses had to make their own fun. They didn't have television, and they didn't have a lot of books or toys. They used the hog's bladder to make a balloon! Would you enjoy playing with it? Why or why not?
- What kind of work do Mary and Laura do to help their parents? How do you help your family?
- Do you think the girls enjoyed Pa's game of mad dog?
- Why must Pa kill a panther or bear on the first try?
- What makes a dog like Prince a good pet?
- Laura received a whittled wooden man, a dress for Charlotte, and five little cakes for her fifth birthday. Would you have liked Laura's birthday gifts when you were five years old?
- When Pa announced the sugar snow, Laura had to have a little taste. Why was she glad no one saw her taste the snow?
- Mrs. Peterson's neighborly kindness created a problem for Laura. If you were Laura, what would you do with your cookie?
- How did Charley lie?
- What did the threshers take as their pay?
- Pa didn't shoot the deer at the end of the book. Why not? What did this show about Pa?

Visitors tour the childhood home of Almanzo Wilder in Malone, New York.
The house is painted red with white trim, just like it was when Almanzo was a boy.
Courtesy of Almanzo & Laura Ingalls Wilder Association, Malone, New York

2

Farmer Boy

BURKE, NEW YORK

Almanzo Wilder lived on his family's farm in Burke, New York, just a few miles from the Canadian border. The Wilders were well known around Burke and the town of Malone. People respected Father, and Mother's butter was the best on the market.

There was always a lot to do on the farm. Almanzo worked hard. He wanted Father to give him even more responsibilities. Most of all, Almanzo wanted to work with Father's beautiful horses.

Almanzo's story in *Farmer Boy* shows us what living on a New York State farm looked like in the 1860s. Farm living was hard, but Almanzo loved it.

HOW THE BOOK CAME TO BE

In this second Little House book, readers learn even more about farming. Most importantly, *Farmer Boy* tells Almanzo Wilder's childhood story.

Almanzo grew up to marry the real Laura Ingalls. And after writing *The Little House in the Big Woods*, Laura wanted to tell a different story. This time she wrote about her husband's life as a boy.

Almanzo and Laura did not know one another as children, so Almanzo told Laura—and their daughter Rose—all about his childhood. Almanzo shared many details to help Laura write the book. He drew careful illustrations of his family farm. He even remembered the length of the barns. The barns were no longer standing when Laura wrote *Farmer Boy*. However, university students and professors found the barns' foundations during a research dig on the Wilder farm in the 1980s. The excavation digs proved Almanzo's drawings were accurate.

Laura and Almanzo's daughter, Rose Wilder Lane, visited the farm when she was an adult. She took notes about the buildings, the land, and even the town. Laura used Rose's research to better imagine the community, and Almanzo's drawings helped her visualize the farm. As readers, we can "see" it all through *Farmer Boy*.

DIG DEEPER

Chapter 1

- Even though he was eight years old, Almanzo had never attended school before. School attendance laws were different in the 1860s, when the events of this book took place.
- Bullies have always been around. Five big boys from Hardscrabble Settlement were the bullies at Almanzo's school. It made Almanzo sick to think of them hurting his teacher.
- Families of students took turns hosting school teachers like Mr. Corse. The families made sure the teacher had a place to stay and meals to eat, a combination that's often called "room and board."
- Corporal punishment uses pain to discipline children. It was common in schools in the United States when Royal and Almanzo were boys and is still legal in some states today.

Chapter 2

- Almanzo thought his father's horses were the best in the country. That didn't mean the whole United States, though; it just meant the region where they lived.
- Almanzo respected his father's hard work, and he trusted him too. He told Father that Big Bill Ritchie attended school that day. His father understood Almanzo's worries about Mr. Corse.
- Today, kitchen pantries typically store unprepared food and kitchen equipment. Long ago, people prepared and stored food in their pantries.
- Alice made an air-castle from straw, which hung over the dining room table. Another name for air-castles is *himmeli*. When translated from German or Swedish, the word relates to "sky" or "heaven." Learn how to make your own air-castle with the Alice's Air-Castle activity (page 30).

Crews reconstructed the barns at the Almanzo Wilder Farm as described *in Farmer Boy.*
Author's collection

FACT OR FICTION?

Could Mother's dress really be so wide it couldn't fit through a doorway? Yes! Hoopskirts made dresses wider than doors!

Women and teenage girls wore hoopskirts to make the bottoms of their dresses wide like a bell. Whalebones or other hard material made the hoopskirts stiff. Women and girls wore multiple petticoats on top of the hoopskirt so the whalebones wouldn't show.

Hoopskirts were fashionable but difficult to wear. A lady couldn't just sit down on a sofa or chair. First she had to gather and lift her hoopskirt, petticoats, and dress. Then she could sit.

The hoopskirt made the dress extra wide at the bottom. Punch *magazine, Wikimedia Commons*

Angeline Wilder loaded these pantry shelves with good food.
Courtesy of Almanzo & Laura Ingalls Wilder Association, Malone, NY

Chapter 3

- Almanzo kept his moccasins soft by rubbing tallow on them every day. Tallow is animal fat. The leather hardened and cracked without it.
- Father got out of bed in the middle of the night. He had to check on the animals in the bitter cold. Running warmed the young cattle's blood. The exercise saved them from freezing to death.

Chapter 4

- As the teacher, Mr. Corse had the authority to discipline the students as he wanted—even with the whip. Mr. Corse was a kind and fair teacher, but he still used the ox-whip to punish the big boys. He didn't want them to hurt any other students or teachers after he left.

Chapter 5

- Father gave Almanzo his own calf-yoke for his birthday. The yoke kept Star and Bright, the oxen calves, paired to work together.
- Farmers trained cows to always go to the same stall in the barn. Stanchions kept the cows in place while the farmer milked them.

ICE HOUSES

After cutting large blocks of ice from lakes during the winter, people stored them in ice houses. These buildings kept the sun's heat away from the ice and were designed to allow melted water to drain away. Later, the blocks of ice were taken to the kitchen, pantry, or cellar area to keep food and drinks cold.

People built ice houses in different ways. Some people dug them into the ground. Others used caves. These types of construction took advantage of the constant underground temperature of 54 degrees Fahrenheit (12°C). Still others built ice houses with wooden planks, stones, or bricks. Some stone walls were several feet thick. With good insulation materials, the ice stayed mostly frozen—even during warm weather. Just like a blanket can keep your body warm at night, the insulation kept the ice cold year-round.

Like the Wilders, many people used sawdust as insulation to keep ice blocks from melting. Wood chips and hay were other popular insulating materials. The insulation wasn't perfect. Ice blocks usually lasted from winter until summer; the ice rarely lasted all year.

Not everyone could cut and store their own ice. People in the South paid to have ice shipped for their ice houses. Others paid to have ice delivered to their homes since they didn't have an ice house. Some families used small buildings built on top of a stream or spring. The spring's cold water kept food (and air) cold instead of ice in the springhouse.

The Wilders had a small, two-shelf cold closet built into their cellar wall. It kept food cold because it was underground.

Workers cut ice to take to an ice house. *National Library of Norway, Wikimedia Commons*

Chapter 8

- Mother sewed all the family's clothes, but she used store-bought fabric for their Sunday best clothes. She wove fabric, called homespun, at home for their other outfits. Machines in factories made full cloth and broadcloth fabrics.

Chapter 9

- Almanzo stayed home from school to train Star and Bright. "Breaking" the calves wasn't painful. It meant the calves were being trained. Almanzo showed kindness and patience even when he was frustrated with them.

Chapter 10

- Father and Almanzo used wooden yokes to carry buckets of maple sap. The shoulder yoke allowed the weight of the buckets to rest on their shoulders. Shoulders are much stronger than hands and fingers.
- The collected maple sap boiled over an outdoor fire. As the water cooked off, they added more sap. The sap darkened when a lot of water evaporated. Then the sap was taken indoors for the final stages of boiling for syrup and sugar. Learn more about making maple syrup on page 4.
- Mother used maple sugar in cooking and baking. Maple sugar would not go bad as quickly as maple syrup. So, it was more important to have than syrup.
- Wintergreen plants grow in the forests of eastern North America. They have red berries. Mother used the leaves to make a minty wintergreen extract. People use wintergreen in medications as well as in foods like mints and gum.
- Potato buyers came from New York City to get potatoes. New York City is in the southern-most part of New York State, about 350 miles (560 km) away from Malone.

Chapter 11

- Alice's hoopskirts got in her way. When Almanzo asked, she *almost* said she wanted to be a boy. Then she realized she could do everything Almanzo did on the farm, plus the things she enjoyed as a girl.
- Before seeds can be planted, a field must be prepared. Fertilizer is spread on a field to make the soil healthy. Animal manure is an excellent fertilizer. It's also free! Plowing digs deep into the soil. It turns the soil over and brings nutrients to the top for the seeds. Plowing also kills unwanted plants and weeds. Harrowing smooths the soil. Marking the soil helped keep rows straight when planting seeds by hand.

Chapter 12

- Mr. Brown was a guest, so his horses had to be looked after. Almanzo fed and watered them in the buggy-house, which was part of the barn.
- Although he was a salesman, Mr. Brown was also a family friend. Look for clues in the chapter that show the good relationship he had with the Wilders.
- Mr. Brown and Mother talked and "argued," but they didn't fight about the tin items. This was just their way of haggling over the price of the tin. Mother paid Mr. Brown in rags instead of money. You can learn more about why Ma paid for tin with rags on page 24.
- People who traveled from town to town selling goods were called peddlers. They loaded their wagons with items to sell. Unfortunately, some peddlers would do anything to make a sale, even tricking and lying to customers. Peddlers like Nick Brown, who visited the same families regularly, had to be honest and fair. Then customers bought from them year after year because they trusted the peddler.

Traveling salesmen called peddlers hauled their merchandise in wagons.
Charles Green Bush, Library of Congress

Chapter 13

- Just as Mother negotiated with the tin peddler, Father bargained with the horse buyer. Negotiations were all about compromise.
- The horse buyers looked in the horses' mouths. A trained person could tell the age of a horse by looking at its teeth. Just like children, horses lose and grow teeth at certain ages.
- Father didn't make the horse buyer feel guilty for not paying what Father wanted for his horses. He invited him to stay for supper, just as if the sale had gone through.
- Father did sell the colts for $200 each. Two hundred dollars in 1860 (just a few years before this story took place) would be worth nearly $3,000 today.

RECYCLED RAGS

Tin peddlers all over New England and beyond sold their wares for rags (scraps of used fabric) instead of cash. Trading and bartering were common.

Why did tin peddlers want rags? They couldn't use them to make their pots and pans, but tin peddlers sold rags to paper mills. The mills needed a way to get rags. The peddlers traveled near and far collecting rags. The mills collected from the tin peddlers, who served as middle men. Then the mills made paper using the cotton and other natural fibers found in the old rags. People even called it rag paper. Later, wood pulp became the popular plant fiber for paper making.

Chapter 14

- Farmers sheared off sheep's wool coat, called fleece, once a year in the spring.
- The Wilders raised sheep and kept them pastured across the road from their house and barns. Merino sheep were known for their good wool.
- Almanzo had the final job of carrying the cut fleece to the upstairs loft. It was the last task to be done, so John was right. Almanzo could not beat Father, John, and Royal—unless he was clever. Almanzo took the last sheep to the loft before it was sheared. The "fleece" waited upstairs before the others sheared it. He did beat them!

Chapter 15

- Each sheep fleece went to a carding machine in Malone. Carding cleaned and straightened the fleece fibers and prepared them for spinning into thread or yarn.
- Alice and Eliza Jane gathered roots and bark from trees. Mother used these to dye wool.

- Baths were typically taken only on Saturdays. However, the family had to prepare to go to town for the Independence Day celebration, so they took a mid-week bath.
- The calendar said July, but it was still cold enough to frost! The family worked hard to save the corn by pouring water on each plant. The water protected the plants from severe damage, even though it froze. The water warmed the plant slowly, but it had to be applied before the sun rose. Without the water, the sun would warm the plants too quickly.

Chapter 16

- Almanzo watched the parade from the Square in Malone at the intersection of Elm and Main Streets. Just as described in the book, it's still triangle-shaped today. See it for yourself in the Visit Malone's Square activity on page 36.
- Cannons were deadly weapons during wartime. To celebrate Independence Day, the cannons were loaded with grass and gunpowder. *Boom!* The cannon went off with a bang, but the grass was much safer than a cannonball.

Chapter 17

- Father threatened to tan Almanzo's jacket if he fooled around with Starlight again. That meant Father would spank or whip Almanzo.
- Rainy days made outdoor work difficult. Father took Almanzo fishing since they couldn't work on the farm.

Chapter 18

- During the restoration of the Wilder home in 1991, workers found a black mark on the parlor wall under six layers of paint and wallpaper. Though we can't be certain, it's possible Almanzo's blacking brush made that mark.

Chapter 19

- The scythes had to be sharpened on the grinding stone before cutting the hay. Sharp tools made work faster and safer.
- Mother called Almanzo to the house with the dinner horn in the middle of the morning. He had to pick up and deliver eggnog to the field workers. The eggnog satisfied their thirst while replacing important nutrients they lost when sweating.
- The butter buyer came from New York City every year. Unlike how she had haggled with the tin peddler, Mother didn't try to bargain with this buyer. She

Oats were placed in small bundles called sheaves.
Bain News Service photograph collection, Library of Congress

expected to earn good money for the butter she had made. The buyer said it was the best he ever saw and paid her fifty cents per pound (0.5 kg). She had 500 pounds (227 kg) of butter. Mother's butter money was an important part of the family income.

Chapter 20

- A bruised apple spoils quickly, so apples had to be picked carefully. Any apple touching a rotten apple also went bad. The saying goes, "One bad apple spoils the bunch."
- After collecting all the perfect apples, Father, Royal, and Almanzo shook more apples from the trees. These apples were collected and quickly pressed for apple cider. Since they weren't stored for the winter, the apples could be imperfect or even bruised.
- Baked potatoes should always be pricked with a knife or fork several times before baking or microwaving. Cooked potatoes build up steam. The pricks from a fork make steam vents that let the steam out slowly. Otherwise, the steam escapes with an explosion.

Chapter 21

- Mules were called a half-breed because they are the offspring of a donkey and a horse.

FACT OR FICTION?

An unnamed American Indian man raced behind the horses. According to the story, he ran one mile in just 2 minutes and 44 seconds. The official world-record holder at the time of publication, Hicham El Guerrouj, ran a mile in 3 minutes and 43 seconds in 1999. That's fast!

The book describes just one lap around the track. Since Malone's track is one-half mile, it's possible he ran a half-mile in under three minutes. That's still fast.

Chapter 23

- When clothing faded, Eliza Jane and Alice carefully took the different pieces of fabric apart, turned them inside out, and sewed them together again. That's how old clothes were reused and made "like new." The Wilders used their clothes as much as possible, even though they could afford new clothes. (The Wilders were not poor; their financial records show the farm made a nice profit.) Most people reused and recycled in the 1800s because it was practical.
- The cobbler who visited the Wilders was never named in *Farmer Boy*. Records show several neighbors worked as shoemakers. It's quite possible the visiting cobbler was one of these neighbors.
- The cobbler was three weeks late. Mother was upset, but she still liked him. The cobbler brought tools (and skills) to make shoes. The Wilders provided leather for the upper parts and wood for the soles and heels. The cobbler spent two weeks making shoes for the whole family.
- The cobbler used waxed thread to sew the shoes together. Wax made the thread glide through the leather more easily. Waxed thread stretched less and resisted water, unlike regular thread.

Chapter 26

- Almanzo had to polish the silverware. Some of it was made of real silver, called sterling silver. Air changes the color of sterling silver, but polishing cleans it. The steel forks and knives rusted when exposed to the air. The scouring-brick removed the rust from the steel. It wasn't nearly as easy as a polishing cloth on silver.

Chapter 27

- Almanzo helped haul wood. When Star and Bright got stuck in the ditch with the empty bobsled, Father drove on by. Pierre, Louis, and Almanzo figured out what to do. Later, when Almanzo's team got stuck while loaded down, Father helped. The load made it a lot tougher to get out of the ditch.
- Almanzo was a smart boy, but he still didn't know enough math to be a farmer. Farmers, then and today, must understand math, along with science. They also need to know how to fix broken equipment and run a business. They should also be experts in what they raise—whether that's animals, crops, or both.

Chapter 29

- Mr. Paddock offered to train Almanzo as a wheelwright apprentice. Almanzo could learn how to build and repair wheels along with carriages and wagons. The idea shocked Mother. Father told his son the advantages and disadvantages of being a shopkeeper, but the decision was Almanzo's. Almanzo finally told Father what he wanted. And Father helped Almanzo be a farmer boy with a special gift.

FACT OR FICTION?

In *Farmer Boy*, Laura Ingalls Wilder introduced us to the Wilder family: James (Father) and Angeline (Mother), Royal, Eliza Jane, Alice, and Almanzo. But the Wilders had six children in the family. Almanzo had two more siblings: an older sister named Laura Ann and a younger brother named Perley.

Why didn't Wilder include Laura Ann and Perley in the story? Because Perley wasn't born yet, and Laura Ann was much older. She was born in 1844 and had already grown up when Almanzo was a boy; she was not a big part of his story. Laura Ann also had the same name as Almanzo's future wife (and author of *Farmer Boy*). It may have confused readers to read about a sister named Laura Wilder when the book was written by Laura Ingalls Wilder.

The Wilder Family from left to right: Royal, Almanzo, James, Perley, Laura Ann, Angeline, Eliza Jane, and Alice. *Photo © Laura Ingalls Wilder Home & Museum, Mansfield, Missouri*

LIVE LIKE ALMANZO

Tin Lantern

After school, Almanzo completed chores in the barn. The barn was dark, so the Wilders used lanterns to see. You can make a tin lantern like Almanzo's with holes that allow the light to shine out.

Adult supervision required.

What You Need

- clean, empty tin can
- permanent marker
- water
- hammer
- nail
- towel
- battery-powered tea light candle

What to Do

1. Remove any glue and labels from your tin can.
2. Use a permanent marker to create a dot design on your tin can. The dots should be about ¼ inch (0.6 cm) apart. A simple design such as a star, letter, or swirl works best. You may want to repeat the design on the back of the can.
3. Fill the can with water and freeze overnight or until solid. Freezing the can of water makes it stable when you pound nails into it.
4. Remove the can from the freezer. Lay the can on a folded towel for a work surface.
5. With an adult's help, place the nail on a mark on your pattern. Gently tap on the nail a few times with the hammer until the can is punctured. Then remove the nail. Repeat the process at another mark on the pattern until you complete the design.
6. Remove the ice by running warm water over the can.
7. If the bottom of the can swelled from freezing, use your hammer to gently tap it flat after the ice is removed.
8. Add an electric tea light. Turn it on to see your design light up.

Alice's Air-Castle

Alice's air-castle hung over the dining room table. She connected pieces of straw to make an interesting decoration. She even added small pieces of fabric to make it extra fancy.

A traditional Finnish holiday craft called *himmeli* uses straw from plants and string to make Christmas ornaments and decorations. Many designs are complicated and use hundreds—or thousands—of straw pieces. Instead of using straw from plants, this craft uses drinking straws. This is a basic design to introduce you to *himmeli*. Once you get the hang of *himmeli*, you can combine short and long straws to make more interesting designs.

What You Need

- drinking straws
- scissors
- thread, at least 4 feet (1 m) long
- scrap fabric (optional)

What to Do

1. Cut drinking straws into 12 equal-length pieces or use 12 full-length straws. If using flexible straws, cut off the flexible tip and use the remaining straw for the project.
2. String three straw pieces on the thread. Form a tight triangle and knot the thread as close as possible to the straws so that they keep their triangular position. Do not cut the thread.

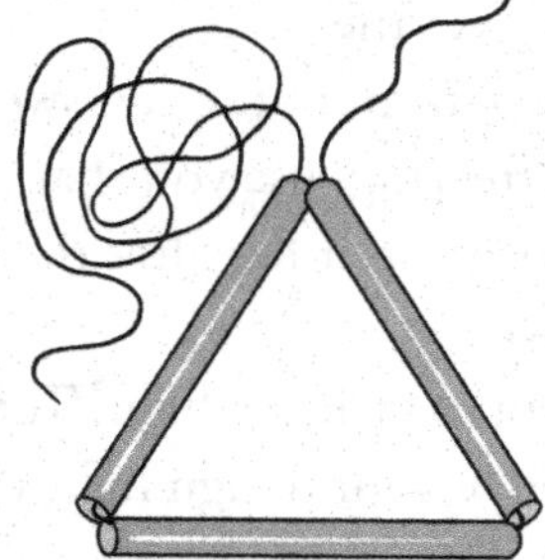

3. Thread two more straw pieces on the long end of the thread. It should form a second triangle. Do not cut the thread.
4. Continue this pattern of adding two straws until you have five connected triangles.

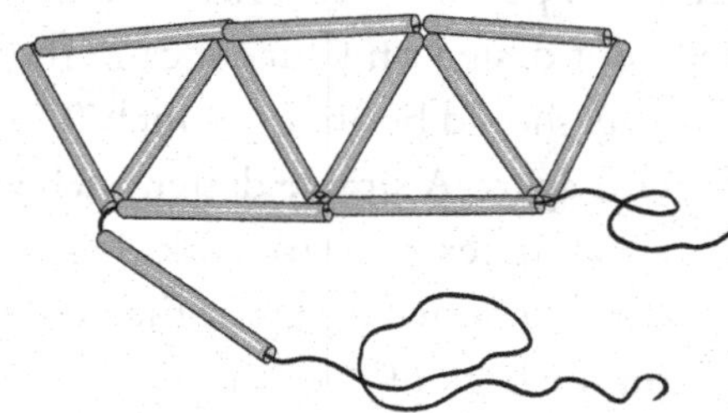

5. Lift the center of the triangle row and add the last straw to make an upright triangle as pictured. It should look like a pyramid with

flat triangles on two sides. Tie the ends together.

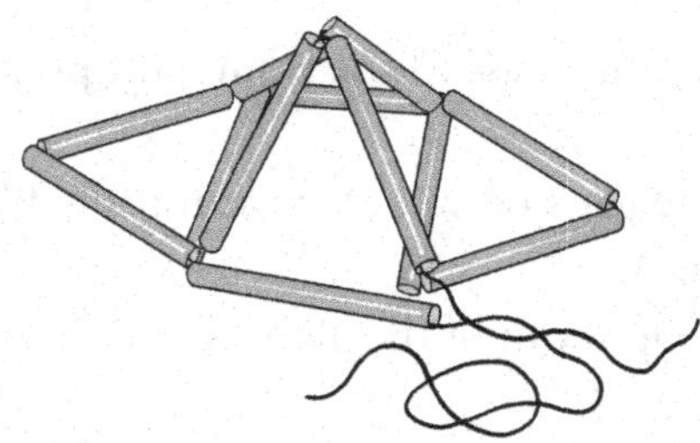

6. Hold the pyramid up. Push the two side triangles down to meet. Cut additional thread to tie these triangles together.

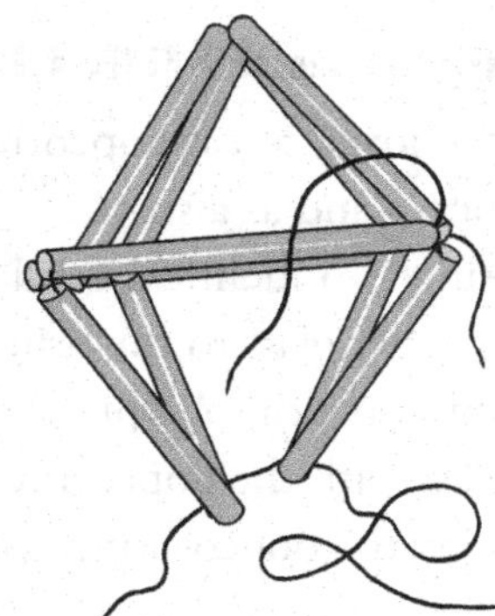

7. Tie a 6- to 10-inch (15- to 25-cm) piece of thread to the air-castle to create a hanging loop. Trim any extra thread pieces that stick out from the air-castle.

Strawberry Jam

The first night the school teacher Mr. Corse stayed with the Wilders, they ate their typical big supper. It included plum preserves, strawberry jam, and grape jelly. Each type of jam or jelly requires a different recipe. This is one way to make strawberry jam. *Adult supervision required.*

What You Need

- 1½ cups (360 mL) sliced strawberries
- ½ cup (120 mL) granulated sugar
- 1 tablespoon (15 mL) fresh lemon juice

What to Do

1. Crush the strawberries into small pieces with a potato masher.
2. Place the strawberries, sugar, and lemon juice in a 10- or 12-inch (25- or 31-cm) skillet. Have an adult bring the strawberry mixture to a boil over medium-high heat. Stir it occasionally.
3. Reduce the heat and cook for 10 to 15 minutes. The mixture should thicken and look like a thick syrup. Remove any foam with a spoon and discard.
4. Place jam in a clean jar (or several if you decide to multiply the recipe). Allow to cool to room temperature, then cover. Keep refrigerated.

Popcorn and Milk Challenge

Almanzo loved to eat popcorn. He also enjoyed combining milk and popcorn as a challenge—and as a snack.

Using two identical drinking glasses, fill one glass to the brim with popcorn. Fill the other glass to the brim with milk.

Add popcorn, one piece at a time, to the glass of milk. Can you really fill the milk glass with the popcorn without spilling?

Enjoy the popcorn using a spoon to scoop it out of the glass.

Apples 'n' Onions

In the ice-house, Royal and Almanzo talked about their favorite foods. They enjoyed their mother's good cooking, but Almanzo liked fried apples 'n' onions the best. Along with roast beef, potatoes, carrots, and turnips, he took four helpings of apples 'n' onions that day.

Apples 'n' onions' flavor might surprise you—in a good way. Try serving this as a snack or with pork as a side dish.

Adult supervision required.

What You Need

- 1 small onion (or half of an onion)
- 3 apples
- 2 tablespoons (30 mL) butter
- 1–2 tablespoons (15–30 mL) brown sugar
- ¼ teaspoon (1 mL) salt
- bacon, cooked and chopped (optional)

What to Do

1. With an adult's help, peel and slice the onion into thin rings. Separate the rings. Set aside.
2. Core and cut the apples into ¼ inch (0.6 cm) wedges.
3. Melt butter over medium heat in a frying pan. Add onion slices. Cook over medium heat until the onions are tender and golden. Stir occasionally.
4. Cover the onions with the apple slices. Sprinkle with brown sugar and salt. Cover the pan with a lid and cook the apples until tender, about 15 to 20 minutes. Remove lid occasionally to stir to prevent

burning. Add a tablespoon (15 mL) of warm water if the apples seem dry.

5. If serving with bacon, stir in the bacon pieces prior to placing the apples 'n' onions in a serving dish.

Self-Turning Old-Fashioned Doughnuts

Mother liked her doughnuts to turn over by themselves so she twisted them. She kept a fresh supply in the doughnut jar for snacking.

Homemade doughnuts do not stay fresh for long. You'll want to enjoy these the same day—or even the same hour—you make them. These old-fashioned doughnuts may be different than the yeast doughnuts from your favorite bakery.

Be careful while making doughnuts; you need to work with an adult for this recipe. The hot oil can spatter and burn you. The doughnuts can also burn quickly in the oil. Wear an apron and oven mitts as needed for protection.

In addition to the safety equipment, you'll need a large pot, slotted spoon, and a kitchen thermometer. An instant thermometer or a candy thermometer that attaches to the side of your pot works best. You'll also want paper towels to drain and cool the doughnuts on.

Adult supervision required.

What You Need

Doughnuts:

- 32–48 ounces (900–1,400 g) shortening (or vegetable oil)
- 2¼ cups (540 mL) all-purpose flour
- ¼ teaspoon (1 mL) baking soda
- 1 teaspoon (5 mL) baking powder
- ¼ teaspoon (1 mL) salt
- ¼ teaspoon (1 mL) nutmeg
- 1 egg
- ½ cup (120 mL) buttermilk*
- 1 tablespoon (15 mL) butter, melted and cooled
- ½ cup (120 mL) granulated sugar

Topping:

- ½ cup (120 mL) granulated sugar
- 2 tablespoons (30 mL) cinnamon

* You can purchase buttermilk or make your own. To make a buttermilk substitute, place 1½ teaspoon (7.5 mL) of white vinegar in a measuring cup. Add milk to fill to the ½ cup (120 mL) line. Allow it to sit for five minutes before adding the buttermilk to the recipe.

What to Do

1. Have an adult scoop the shortening into a large pot over medium

heat. (You can also use a deep fryer.) Slowly adjust the temperature, if needed, to keep the temperature between 365°F and 375°F (185°C and 190° C) while cooking. It takes time for the shortening to melt and to reach this temperature. Do *not* use high heat. Monitor the temperature of the oil.

2. Mix together the flour, baking soda, baking powder, salt, and nutmeg in a bowl. Set aside.
3. In a large bowl, beat the egg, buttermilk, melted butter, and sugar together.
4. Quickly stir the flour mixture into the wet ingredients. Allow the dough to rest for 5 minutes. Add 1 tablespoon (15 mL) of flour if mixture is too sticky to handle.
5. Sprinkle flour on a large, clean work surface. Place the dough on the flour. Knead the dough a couple of times.
6. Check the temperature of the oil. Adjust the heat as needed to keep the temperature between 365°F and 375°F (185°C and 190°C).
7. Prepare a cookie sheet with parchment paper or lightly sprinkle it with flour. This will be where you set the doughnuts before frying them. The parchment paper (or sprinkled flour) will prevent them from sticking to the cookie sheet.
8. With well-floured hands (or a floured rolling pin), flatten the dough until it is between ¼ and ½ inch (0.6 and 1.3 cm) thick. With a floured knife, cut dough strips that are about 6 inches (15 cm) long and 1 inch (2.5 cm) wide.

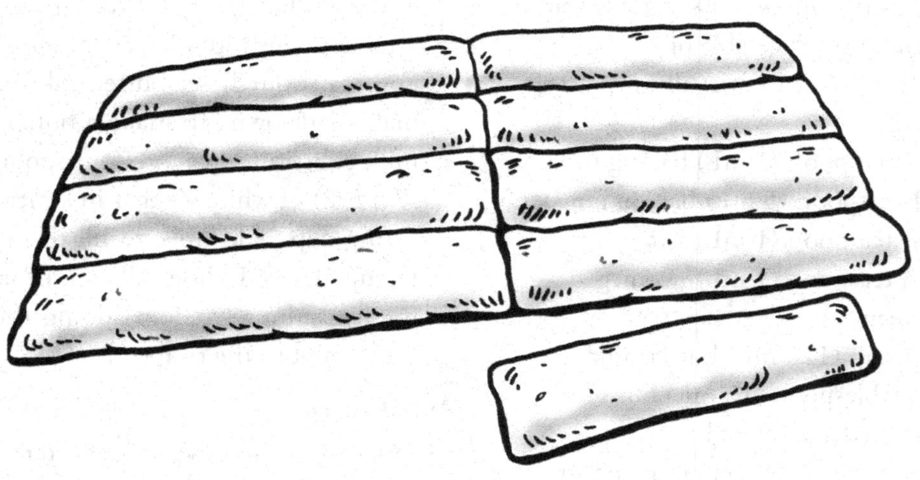

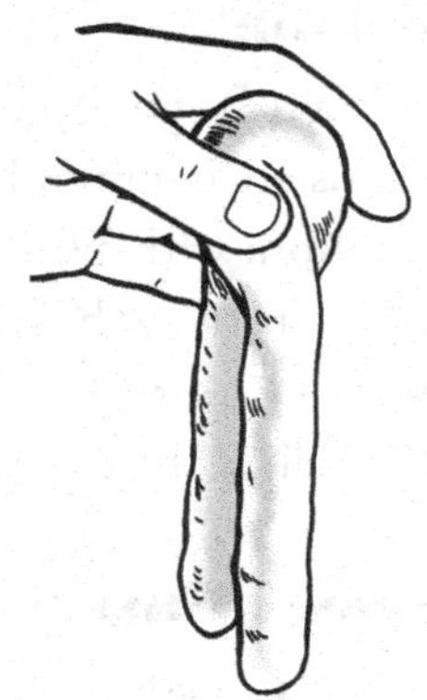

9. Take each strip of dough and roll it into a 10-inch (25-cm) rope. Fold the rope in half (as illustrated), then twist the folded halves to create a sort of braid. Pinch the two twisted halves together at the ends and place on the prepared cookie sheet. Repeat this process for the rest of the doughnuts. You can also make doughnut holes with scraps of dough by cutting any extra strips into one-inch pieces.
10. For the topping combine the ½ cup (120 mL) of sugar and 2 tablespoons (30 mL) of cinnamon together and set aside.
11. Carefully slide one doughnut off a large spoon and into the melted shortening. After about two minutes, it should be brown on both sides. The doughnut may not turn over by itself if it isn't twisted enough. If it is browned on the bottom, you can flip the doughnut using a large spoon. If it takes longer than three minutes to cook, your shortening is not hot enough.
12. Use tongs or the slotted spoon to remove the doughnut from the melted shortening. Dip and roll it in the cinnamon and sugar mixture. Then place it on a plate covered in paper towels.
13. Continue cooking doughnuts. You can cook a couple at a time but do not overcrowd the pot.
14. Serve the doughnuts freshly made for the best texture and flavor.

FLOUR MEASUREMENT

The way you measure flour can change the texture of the food you're making. Doughnuts, bread, cakes, and cookies all become too dry if you use too much flour.

When measuring dry ingredients like flour or sugar, you want to use measuring cups labeled with the exact amount needed on them. They're meant to be filled to the top. (Liquid measuring cups have a pour spout. You fill them only to the measurement marked on the side.) When you measure flour, scoop the flour with a spoon and sprinkle it into the measuring cup. Then, use the flat edge of a butter knife and scrape it across the measuring cup's rim. This "levels" the flour to the exact measurement.

Never tap on a measuring cup of flour or push on it with a spoon to pack it in. Doing either of these will make your measuring cup too full of flour and change how your food tastes.

Giddap!

Star and Bright eagerly followed Almanzo's voice as he taught them. Voice commands are commonly used with horses, oxen, and even sled dogs.

Work with a friend to practice the commands of "giddap" (go), "whoa" (stop), "haw" (turn to the left), and "gee" (turn to the right). Take turns making an obstacle course for each other. The person who makes the course is the trainer who commands the other where to go. How well do you follow instructions?

Grass Whistle

Almanzo made a whistle with a piece of grass, but Alice could only whistle with her mouth. With practice, you can also whistle with grass. Not all grass works well for grass whistles; experiment with several blades of grass.

What to Do

1. Choose a blade of grass that is thick and sturdy. It should also be about ½ inch (1 cm) wide and at least 6 inches (15 cm) long.
2. Place your thumbs side by side with the blade of grass in between them.
3. Use your fingertips to pull the grass tight while keeping a small crack between your thumbs.
4. Blow into the crack between your thumbs. Air should move over the grass creating a whistling sound, but it may take several tries.
5. Adjust the blade of grass and size of the crack to change the sound of the whistle.

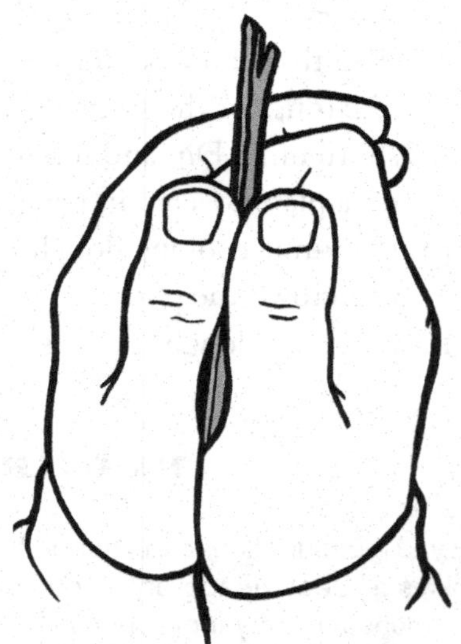

Visit Malone's Square

Use Google Earth or another website that uses satellite images to let viewers see intersections and buildings along roads. Search for the intersection of Main Street and Elm Street in Malone, New York. Can you see the triangular-shaped

"Square" where Almanzo watched the Independence Day parade? Explore what the town looks like today. It's changed a lot! Can you find the fairgrounds?

Pink Lemonade

A man sold a glass of pink lemonade for five cents to Frank. Almanzo decided to save Father's money instead of buying the tasty drink.

You can make your own pink lemonade at home.

What You Need

- 9 cups (2160 mL) water
- 2 cups (480 mL) freshly squeezed lemon juice (from 15 to 18 lemons)
- ½ cup (120 mL) cranberry juice
- 2 cups (480 mL) granulated sugar

What to Do

1. In a large pitcher combine the water, lemon juice, cranberry juice, and sugar. Stir to dissolve sugar.
2. Chill in the refrigerator. Serve over ice.

Homemade Ice Cream

When Father and Mother visited Uncle Andrew, they left the children behind. The kids made ice cream right away. You won't need to hand crank your ice cream to mix it, but you will have to shake it. Use this recipe to make one serving of ice cream.

What You Need

- ½ cup (120 mL) heavy cream or half-and-half
- 1 tablespoon (15 mL) granulated sugar
- ¼ teaspoon (1 mL) vanilla
- 2 quart-sized freezer bags
- 1 gallon-sized freezer bag
- 3–4 cups (720–960 mL) ice
- ⅓ cup rock salt
- towel or mittens (optional)

What to Do

1. Place the cream, sugar, and vanilla in a quart-size bag. Remove as much air as possible and seal the bag tightly. Then check the seal again. Squeeze the bag several times to mix the ingredients together.
2. Place the bag with the cream mixture in the other quart-size bag. Seal that bag. Double-check its seal as well.
3. Place the ice in the gallon-sized bag. Sprinkle the rock salt on the ice. Place the sealed bag of ice cream ingredients inside the gallon-sized bag with the ice and salt, then seal the gallon-sized bag.
4. Squeeze and shake the whole bag until the ice cream thickens. It may take more than 15 minutes. Use the towel or mittens to keep your hands warm while you work.
5. Remove the small bag once the cream mixture seems to be the right texture. Enjoy the ice cream right from the baggie with a spoon.

HOUSE TALK

- After their big supper, the Wilders spent an evening eating apples and popcorn and drinking cider. Reading and quiet activities entertained the family. How would you spend your evenings if you didn't have electricity?
- Mr. Ritchie was proud his son could thrash and hurt teachers. How could have Mr. Ritchie influenced Big Bill Ritchie's behavior?
- Do you think it was more important for Almanzo to attend school or to help with farm work? Why?
- Star and Bright pulled the sled, but it didn't go as Almanzo planned. Was he successful at breaking the calves?
- What did Father think of Almanzo's fleece joke? How could you tell?
- Almanzo wore his suit, including a vest and coat, to the Independence Day celebration in town. Why did Almanzo and the family dress up? How do you dress for community events?

- Cousin Frank dared Almanzo to ask Father for a nickel for pink lemonade. Father explained that earning money is hard work. How is that still true today?
- Almanzo tried to hurry nature. He wanted to grow up even faster so he could break the colts. Can eating more help you grow faster? Does it matter what you eat?
- The children enjoy their time alone without Mother and Father first by making ice cream and eating watermelon. What would you do first if you were left home alone?
- When Eliza Jane bossed Almanzo he threw the blacking brush at her. Whose fault was the mark on the wall? Why did Eliza Jane repair the wallpaper?
- Do you think a person could really run a full mile in less than three minutes?
- Almanzo worried his first-prize ribbon was earned unfairly. Was he right to tell the judge his pumpkin's secret? Why?
- The farm boys beat the town boys in the physical contests at the fair. Why do you think the farm boys would win more often than the town boys?
- Almanzo helped make candles using tallow. Why did they make candles right after butchering time?
- On Christmas Eve, Royal and Almanzo hung socks and the girls hung stockings. How do you know these were their every-day socks and stockings instead of stockings used just once a year like we do today?
- The children hadn't noticed the time when they woke up on Christmas morning. How could you tell Father didn't really mind being awakened early?
- Father let Almanzo take charge of selling the hay. Did Almanzo do well selling the hay? How do you know?
- When Almanzo returned the pocketbook and money, Mr. Thompson nearly called Almanzo a thief. Mr. Paddock wouldn't allow that. Mr. Paddock forced Mr. Thompson to give Almanzo $200. Should honesty be rewarded? Why did Father let Almanzo keep the money?
- Mr. Paddock offered to teach Almanzo all about the buggy and wheel business through an apprenticeship. The business could even be Almanzo's one day. Why did Mr. Paddock choose Almanzo?
- How did Father help Almanzo be a farmer boy?

An 1860s covered wagon sits beside the first replica log cabin of the Little House on the Prairie Museum. *Courtesy of Little House on the Prairie Museum; Independence, Kansas*

3

Little House on the Prairie

INDEPENDENCE, KANSAS

The Big Woods were getting too crowded for Pa. The Ingalls family packed up their wagon and left their cozy cabin. They set out for Indian Territory.

Pa found the perfect spot to settle down in the tall grasses of the prairie. He liked the rich soil for farming. Many wild animals lived there, which was important for hunting. Log by log, Pa built a small cabin. A neighbor helped build the stable. Another neighbor helped to dig the well.

But living on the prairie wasn't as simple as the Ingalls family had hoped. They built their home in Indian Territory—where no white settlers were supposed to live! The Osage (pronounced oh-SAGE) tribe of American Indians lived just a couple of miles away. It was a stressful time for the settlers and the Osage.

While the Ingalls family lived on the Osage's land, peace with the tribe was very important. What would the family have to do to stay on good terms with their neighbors? Should they stay in Indian Territory?

A FAMILY HISTORY

Little House on the Prairie was published in 1935. It is likely Laura Ingalls Wilder's most popular book and shares her family's story of living in Indian Territory. Today we know the Ingalls family lived on the Osage Diminished Reserve in Kansas.

Laura was young but smart enough to understand that her family had moved to land that belonged to someone else. Even its nickname—Indian Territory or Indian country—told who owned it. Laura tried to question her parents about why the Indians had to move west, but Ma and Pa left her confused. They didn't have a good reason for living there.

Laura Ingalls Wilder wrote her family's story realistically. American Indians made Ma uncomfortable. Wilder didn't avoid prejudice when she recounted her childhood. Wilder shared enough with readers to help us think deeper about the relationships between the white settlers and the native population. In the book, Pa disagreed with others' negative comments about the Indians. He explained why many American Indians might have a reason to hate white settlers. He said they had been moved west so many times that it was only natural that they resented the settlers.

Laura Ingalls Wilder could have edited the characters' attitudes to make them kinder in *Little House on the Prairie*. Instead, Wilder depicted racial prejudice in her books because she saw and heard it as a child.

When others don't speak your same language or look different than you, it's easy to be scared. But if you learn about new cultures, you can make new friends. Get to know people and form your own opinions.

Dig deep into history. Learn more about what motivated people to do what they did. Laura Ingalls Wilder shared her family's perspective in the Little House books. She didn't tell readers how or what to believe. Instead, she let readers like you decide what to think.

We change and grow as a country and people. When we do, we realize the ways people lived and thought in the past weren't always right. We can learn from the past and make changes in ourselves.

As you read *Little House on the Prairie*, try to consider both sides of the story: the Ingalls family's side and that of the Osage American Indians.

HOW THE WEST WAS WON

The US government encouraged the idea of Manifest Destiny. Though Manifest Destiny isn't named in *Little House on the Prairie*, the book hints at the idea, especially in the chapters "Pa Goes to Town" and "The Tall Indian." Manifest Destiny was the belief that the US territories should expand west across North America. Farmers needed more land to grow America's food. And more land would give the United States more power and more influence in the world.

But native people already lived on the western lands, and they wanted to keep it. Their ancestors had lived there far longer than the European settlers.

Soon white (European) settlers moved west. Some settlers and American Indians lived peacefully as neighbors. But not all of them. The hostility between the settlers and native people was very real. Settlers invaded the Indians' land, and the US government forced the Indians to move repeatedly.

The government also made legal agreements, called treaties, with the American Indians. The US government broke hundreds of treaties. Sometimes that meant American Indians sold their homes and land to the United States but were never paid. Other times the government tried to pay in food and other items instead of money. The government even tried to tell the American Indians when and how they could use their own money because some officials didn't think the native people would spend it "wisely."

When the United States bought their land, the American Indians were sent to designated areas called reservations. Only members of the relocated tribes—and others who had permission—were supposed to live on reservations. Some white settlers moved to reservations anyway.

The settlers and American Indians both defended what was important to them. The American Indians wanted to keep their land. Settlers and natives both feared for their lives, not knowing when or if a fight or battle would happen.

Today, there are about 300 American Indian reservations and land areas in the United States. US state and federal governments have limited authority there. Instead, the local nations (tribes) control and govern the reservations.

DIG DEEPER

Chapter 1

- The family had to cross multiple rivers to get from their old home in Wisconsin to Kansas. They were the Mississippi, Missouri, and Verdigris Rivers. The Mississippi River was frozen. It was like a natural ice bridge for them to cross. Once the ice thawed, the river would be too high and wide to cross safely.
- Mustangs are small, strong horses. Sometimes they even live in the wild—without any human care. When mustangs are trained and well cared for, like Pet and Patty, they can be exceptional horses.

Chapter 2

- The creek rose so fast it took Pa by surprise. He jumped into the cold creek to calm Pet and Patty. If he hadn't, they would have had big problems. The creek likely would have taken the wagon downstream, even though horses swim. It's also a possibility the wagon could roll over and trap the family under water.

Chapter 3

- Fenced pastures weren't possible when pioneers were on the move. A stake in the ground with a long rope attached to the animal let it eat grass without wandering off. It's called a picket line.

Chapter 4

- Laura was curious about the American Indians. She didn't understand why Ma didn't like them or why the family had moved to Indian Territory. So she asked. Ma didn't give a good answer why she didn't like their neighbors, but she explained that Pa heard the land would open up to settlers soon. This was because the government often moved the American Indians off of reservations so settlers could move in. Even so, the land wasn't open to the settlers. It belonged to the native people, and white settlers like the Ingallses were not supposed to live there.

Chapter 6

- Pa mentioned his Indian neighbors might be away on a hunting trip. The Osage went on two buffalo hunts each year.

Chapter 7

- Imagine two adults living in a house just 8 feet (2.4 m) wide! Measure the length and width of your bedroom for comparison.

Chapter 8

- Pa used a chain and lock to keep anyone from stealing Pet and Patty. Locks had been around for many centuries before pioneer days, but they became smaller, stronger, and more portable in the 18th and 19th centuries.

Chapter 9

- Pa tried to tame his hair with bear grease before he and Ma were married. Think of it like a natural hair gel.

Chapter 10

- During the part of history called the Victorian Era (named for Queen Victoria's reign in England from 1837–1901), many white women liked to keep their skin pale. Though Ma was a pioneer and far from the cities, she kept up with fashion trends. She wanted her girls to wear their bonnets to keep the sun off their faces. Today people with all skin tones use hats and sunscreen to do the same thing—not because of fashion, but to protect their skin from sunburns.
- Pa carefully chose straight trees to build the house. He stacked the logs, but they had cracks between them. Pa used small pieces of wood and a mud plaster to fill in the cracks. This was called chinking.

The Laura Ingalls Wilder replica log cabin was built in 2018 in Independence, Kansas. *Courtesy of Little House on the Prairie Museum; Independence, Kansas*

Chapter 11

- The Osage visitors didn't go to the house to scare the family. They wanted food. They *needed* food. Their ribs showed. They ate every bit of Ma's corn bread—even the tiny crumbs that fell to the floor. It's possible they were more than hungry—they may have been starving.

Chapter 13

- Pa helped the cowboys keep the cattle out of the creek beds and ravines. Instead of paying Pa with cash, the cowboys agreed to give Pa a piece of beef. Bartering, or trading goods or work, was often more important to the pioneers than cash. Pa brought home the expected beef *and* a cow *and* a calf too. The cow's milk gave them extra nutrition in their diets. Since the family usually ate wild game, the beef was a nice change.

Chapter 15

- Today we call fever 'n' ague malaria. The Ingalls family recovered from the illness thanks to Dr. Tan's treatment. He gave them the bitter-tasting medicine called quinine. Pa was right to eat that watermelon. Malaria spreads through the bites of some mosquitoes—not ripe watermelon. Malaria is still a problem today, though quinine treats it. About a million people still die in Africa from malaria every year. In some African villages and towns, it is hard to afford or get medicine.
- Laura was in awe of her doctor. It is quite possible that in Laura's childhood she had never seen a black man before Dr. Tan. The real man Laura Ingalls Wilder described, Dr. George Tann, was born in Pennsylvania in 1835. He lived about 2 miles (3 km) from the Ingalls family in Indian Territory. Dr. Tann served his neighbors, including the Osage, as a doctor.

TEXAS LONGHORNS

Just as their name implies, the hardy breed of cattle called Texas longhorns are known for their long horns. From tip to tip, many females' horns are often 70 or 80 inches (180 or 200 cm) in length, but they can be shorter or longer. Bulls' and steers' horns are even longer. The current record holder is 125¾ inches (319 cm) from tip to tip. That's more than 10 feet (300 cm) wide!

Longhorns can thrive in environments where other cattle can't. They eat a variety of plants—even weeds and brush. Their diet certainly helped Texas longhorns thrive on the prairie.

Cowboys drove the cattle north. There the cattle were loaded onto trains and shipped farther north where beef was hard to buy.

Chapter 16

- A burning stick rolled under Mary's chair and scared her. Laura's quick thinking made her pull the rocking chair, with Mary and Carrie in it, to safety. Fear sometimes paralyzes a person. Other times it makes us incredibly brave—and strong.
- After the chimney fire, Pa planned to rebuild the chimney with "green" sticks. Green wood is freshly cut. It has moisture in it and does not burn easily.

Chapter 18

- Pa's Osage visitor tried to speak to Pa once he knew Pa was friendly. Pa thought the visitor spoke French. Many American Indians knew multiple languages in addition to their tribal language. Some learned French, English, and other languages from settlers, trappers, and other native tribes.
- Pa planned to sell and trade his furs for a plow. He was thankful the furs weren't taken since they were his main way to earn money.

- Two Osage neighbors went to the Ingallses' home. They took food and tobacco and almost stole Pa's furs. Since the white settlers had arrived, animals weren't as plentiful to hunt for food. The Osage might have thought taking food and belongings from the settlers was like getting paid rent to live on their land—especially if they were desperate for food and other essential items.

Chapter 22

- Pa fought the prairie fire with fire! Backfires are deliberately set to stop wildfires. Pa's fire burned the dry grass that would have fed the prairie fire. The smaller backfire moved toward the wildfire and consumed any fuel in its path. Pa also plowed a row of soil called a furrow. Plowing buried the grass under the soil. Eventually, without grass fuel, the wildfire sputtered out.
- Mr. Scott and Mr. Edwards didn't like their American Indian neighbors. Pa defended the Indians, saying they likely just wanted to be left alone. Their hate for the white settlers made sense to Pa. He thought it was because they had been forced to move west so many times. Though Pa understood the American Indians' anger, he had moved to their land illegally. He was part of the problem.

THE UNITED STATES–DAKOTA WAR OF 1862

Four young, hungry men from the Dakota tribe (also known by white settlers as Sioux, though the Dakota found that name insulting) stole eggs from a Minnesota farm in August 1862. A fight broke out with the chicken owner, and five white settlers in that family were killed. Expecting an attack from the United States because of the deaths, the leaders of the Dakota chose to fight right away. They didn't want to wait to be attacked.

Why did the Dakota want to fight? It wasn't just to protect the young men who killed the settlers. They used the war to try to remind the US government to follow through on its broken treaties. The Dakota were still waiting on promised food and money. They had been lied to and forced to move around for years.

It was a fierce war. Between 400 and 600 white soldiers and settlers died, including women and children. Unfortunately, historians do not know how many Dakota were killed.

The war was short, just six weeks long, but people didn't forget it quickly. It was known by many names including the Dakota Conflict, the United States–Dakota War of 1862, and the Sioux Uprising. Some even called it the Minnesota Massacre, like the adults did in *Little House on the Prairie*.

Chapter 23

- Pa heard another rumor. Now the gossip was that settlers were preparing for a stockade. A stockade was built for protection, especially before a war. A supply of weapons were kept in stockades. Sometimes families and soldiers would live in a stockade like a small community. Even if the news wasn't true, the neighboring Osage could have heard it too. A stockade—or a stockade rumor—could have made a bad situation even worse.
- Laura Ingalls Wilder's research led her to believe Le Soldat du Chêne was the American Indian peacemaker from her childhood, so she included his name in the book. Le Soldat du Chêne was a real Osage Indian chief and friendly with the white settlers. Today, however, researchers know it is unlikely he was the peacemaking chief discussed in *Little House on the Prairie*.

Chapter 25

FACT OR FICTION?

Laura Ingalls Wilder wrote how her family lay awake at night listening to the drumming and yelling of their Osage neighbors. She called the loud yells a war cry, but she (and her family) might have misunderstood what was happening.

Some experts think the Osage were getting ready to move since records show they had just signed a treaty. They would have mourned the idea of leaving behind the graves of their ancestors. Before going to their new reservation, they would go on a buffalo hunt, which might explain the "war cry."

- Pa suggested Mr. Edwards wouldn't be safe if he went down the Verdigris River because American Indians might attack. Pa no longer defended his Indian neighbors because he was angry that he had to move. He seemed to forget he was never given permission to live there and never purchased the land. Pa didn't realize that when the Osage left, they had left for good.
- Pa dug up Ma's garden potatoes. They wouldn't be able to start a new garden in time for the growing season at their new home, so they didn't keep them as seed potatoes. They ate them.

Chapter 26

- The Ingalls family, like many pioneer families, packed and moved quickly. They didn't own much. Pa and Ma didn't have a plan of where to go next.

THE OSAGE INDIANS

Like many Plains Indians, the Osage were seminomadic. That means they had permanent homes but also took long hunting trips. They farmed, foraged, and hunted in and near their villages. They also left their villages for long bison (buffalo) hunts each year, eventually returning home when the hunt was over.

The government first made the Osage leave their land, located in present-day Arkansas and Missouri, in 1808. In chapter 24, the Ingalls family watched them ride away. They would not return—it was another government relocation. This was likely in 1870. Today about 20,000 members of the Osage remain.

A camp of the Osage nation. *O. Drum, Library of Congress*

LIVE LIKE LAURA

Cracked Ice

During the night, a loud noise awakened Laura from her sleep. Ma told Laura it was just the river's ice cracking. Ice cracked as it melted and was surprisingly loud.

What You Need

- ice cubes
- 2 plastic bowls (medium and large sizes)
- water
- freezer
- sink

What to Do

1. Fill the large plastic bowl about two-thirds of the way full. Freeze it overnight to make a giant ice cube.
2. The next day, fill the medium bowl most of the way with warm water.
3. Add ice cubes to the bowl and listen closely. Do you hear them cracking?
4. Remove the giant ice cube from the freezer. Run a little warm water on the outside of the bowl so you can easily remove the ice from the bowl.
5. Fill a sink with a several inches of warm water. Now put the giant ice cube in the sink and listen. Did you hear the ice cracking? How were the sounds compared to the ice cubes? Imagine having just crossed the Mississippi River and hearing the ice cracking.

Fire Starter

When the family stopped the wagon, they made a fire. Pa carefully prepared the ground and collected fuel and water. Ma cooked over the fire.

Follow Pa's lead and build your own campfire with an adult's help. Collect only wood from branches that are on the ground. Fresh wood does not burn well. *Adult supervision required.*

What You Need

- tinder (dry grass, dry pine needles, birch bark, wood chips, cotton balls, or newspaper strips)
- kindling (twigs, about 1 inch [2.5 cm] wide)

- firewood
- water
- matches or lighter

What to Do

1. With an adult's help, prepare a grill, fireplace, or fire pit. Keep these safety warnings in mind as you work:
   - Do not build a fire on concrete or paved driveways or roads. Fire damages these surfaces.
   - Do not build a fire in dry conditions or under trees or branches.
   - Keep a bucket of water on hand in case any sparks escape the designated fire area.
2. In the center of a sand or dirt ring, place several handfuls of tinder in a loose pile. The tinder catches fire quickly, but the flames do not last long.
3. Build a "tepee" of small twigs over the tinder. Thin sticks are the fire's kindling.
4. Fire always burns in an upward direction. With an adult, light the tinder at the bottom.
5. When the kindling burns strong, place two or three pieces of firewood on the fire in another loose "tepee" shape. Be careful not to smother the kindling. Air needs to move around the wood.
6. Relax by your fire or use it as a cookfire.
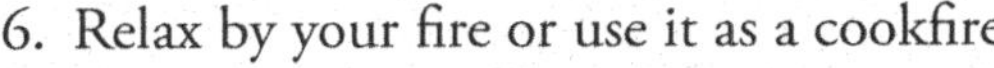
7. Use water to put out the fire.

Outdoor Laundry

Pa brought Ma water from the creek to wash clothes. Afterward, she spread them out on the grass to dry. A long time ago people washed laundry in natural water sources like creeks. (We now know doing this is bad for the wildlife who live there.)

You can try washing your own clothes too. It's best to wash laundry on a warm, sunny day so that any spills and splashes dry quickly.

What You Need

- portable tub or bucket
- water
- laundry soap
- washboard or large, clean stone
- dirty laundry (socks and washcloths work well)

What to Do

1. Take your washtub or bucket outside and fill it with water. Add about 1 teaspoon (5 mL) of laundry soap. Use your hand and arm to stir the soap into the water. (Note: laundry soap does not typically make water sudsy.)
2. Place your washboard or stone in the tub. Then put your laundry in the tub.
3. Wash the clothes, one at a time, by rubbing them along the washboard or the stone.
4. When all the clothes are washed, empty the tub and fill it with clean water. Rinse the clothes in the clean water. Wring them out and spread them in the grass or even on bushes to dry.
5. After the clothes dry completely, shake and fold the items before putting them away.

Log House Craft

Pa built the family a simple log house. He began by cutting down trees in the creek bottoms and hauling the logs home. Notches in the logs made it so they would set on top of one another and not roll off as he built the walls. Pa even built his own door and cut long slabs to cover the roof.

Design and build your own edible log cabin. It won't take as long as building a real log cabin, but it's important to take your time. These directions will get you started, but you'll need to use your imagination to make the log cabin uniquely yours.

What You Need

- pretzel rods (1 tub)
- flat tray, platter, or cardboard
- frosting (2 cans)
- frosting bag with tip (optional)*
- graham crackers (1 box)
- square cereal or crackers, like Rice Chex or Wheat Thins (optional)

* If you don't have a frosting bag, you can use a knife to spread the frosting. However, if you want to make a frosting bag, it's easy. Place the frosting in the corner of a baggie. Snip the corner off but be sure not to cut off too much. Now you can make lines of frosting on the log cabin by gently squeezing the bag.

What to Do

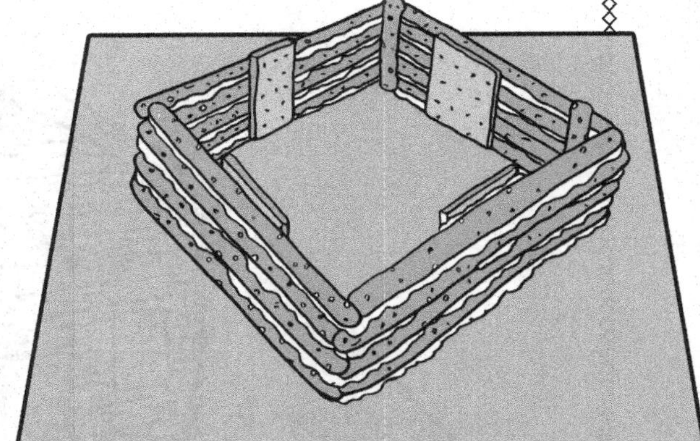

1. Place four pretzel rods on a tray to make a square. Secure the pretzels to the tray with frosting.
2. Spread frosting on top of each pretzel log using a frosting bag or knife. This is the "mortar" that holds the house together. After placing a few more "logs," allow the frosting to set for about 15 minutes. Add graham cracker reinforcements to the interior of the walls (which won't be visible once the house is complete).
3. Repeat placing the "logs" and "mortar" until the walls are full height. Add more reinforcements inside the cabin as needed.
4. Add a door and windows using graham crackers. Attach them with frosting mortar.

5. On opposite sides of the house, build two walls with central peaks, stacking pretzels from longest to shortest. Each stacked pretzel in these peaks should be slightly smaller than the one below it. Both peaks should use the same number of pretzel rods. Allow the walls to dry overnight before adding the roof.
6. Build a roof using graham crackers as a base. Reinforce the underside of the roof with pretzel rods. Allow it to set for 15 minutes before attaching it to the house with frosting mortar.
7. You can add cereal squares or crackers to add "shingles" to the rooftop. Secure everything in place with more frosting mortar.
8. For fun, add a chimney made with graham crackers too.

Living Light Test

People breathe oxygen, and fire needs oxygen too. Pa tested the air quality of the well with a simple candle test. If there isn't enough oxygen, the candle's flame goes out.

Mr. Scott didn't understand the importance of the candle test, so he went into the well without the candle. He passed out! The bottom of the well didn't have enough oxygen in it. Pa saved his life by taking him to fresh air.

Use this test to see how the candle flame uses oxygen.

Adult supervision required.

What You Need

- tea light or small candle
- matches or lighter
- clear jar or glass
- stopwatch or clock with a second hand (optional)

What to Do

1. Place the candle on a heat-resistant surface. With an adult's help, light the candle with the matches or lighter.
2. Turn the jar upside down and use it to cover the candle.
3. See how many seconds it takes for the candle's flame to go out.
4. When the candle's flame is extinguished, remove the glass jar.

Dried Berries

Laura and Ma picked pails full of ripe blackberries. The family ate as much as they wanted, and Ma dried the rest in the sun. Dried berries were a sweet treat in the winter when fresh fruit wasn't available.

What You Need

- blueberries or blackberries
- baking tray or cookie sheet with sides
- clear jar with lid
- cheesecloth or other thin cloth (optional)
- oven (optional)
- parchment paper (optional)

What to Do

It's difficult to say how long it will take to dry berries because some berries are juicier or bigger than others. The moisture in the air, called humidity, also changes drying times even when the sun shines brightly. Because of this, it's often best to dry the berries in an oven. However, both of these methods will dry your berries. Whichever method you try, it's best to start drying berries in the morning because it takes a long time. When drying berries in the sunshine, choose low-humidity days.

Sunshine Drying

1. Remove all stems.
2. Place the berries on a baking tray or cookie sheet so they are close together, but not touching.
3. Cover the tray with cheesecloth to keep curious insects away.
4. Set it in the sun. It may take several (or many) days to dry completely. Stir once daily. Bring the tray indoors when the sun sets or before dew gets on the berries. Return them to the sun until they appear dry and wrinkled—like raisins. Test for moisture by squeezing a berry. If no juice appears, go on to step 5. Continue drying if any wetness appears.
5. Fill a jar about ¾ of the way with the dried berries. Close the lid tightly. Gently shake the jar daily, but do not open it. If any moisture appears on the jar, the berries are not completely dry, and you'll need to return to Step 4 (or try the oven-drying method for a shortened amount of time).
6. Once they're completely dry, enjoy the berries by themselves or with cereal, yogurt, or granola.

Oven Drying

Adult supervision required.

1. Preheat the oven to 200°F (95°C).
2. Remove all stems.
3. Line the baking tray with parchment paper. Place the berries on the parchment paper so they are close together, but not touching.
4. With the help of an adult, place them in the preheated oven. Gently stir them every two hours.
5. It will take many hours for the berries to dry in the oven. If you need to go to bed (or leave the house) before the berries are dry, leave the berries in the oven with the door closed and turn off the oven. The next day remove the berry tray from the oven before preheating. Then begin the process again.

6. Return the berries to the oven until they appear dry and wrinkled—like raisins. Test for moisture by squeezing a berry. If no juice appears, go to Step 7. Continue drying if any wetness appears.
7. Fill a jar about ¾ of the way with the dried berries. Close the lid tightly. Gently shake the jar daily, but do not open it. This "conditions" the berries. If any moisture appears on the jar, the berries are not completely dry and you'll need to go back to Step 6.
8. Once they're completely dry, enjoy the berries by themselves or with cereal, yogurt, or granola.

Hide the Thimble

Laura and Mary spent more time indoors during the winter than during other seasons. They amused themselves with simple games like Hide the Thimble.

The game is a bit like hide-and-seek, but it's played in a small space like a cabin, bedroom, or classroom. Two or more players are needed for this game.

What You Need

- thimble or another small object

What to Do

Take turns hiding the thimble. One friend hides it, and the other friend finds it!

You can also give clues to the seeker with "hot" and "cold" hints. Say, "You're getting warmer" when the seeker is near the thimble. When the seeker is far away, announce, "You're ice cold!" or "You're freezing!"

Cat's Cradle

Cat's cradle is a game for two players. The players pass a loop of yarn or string back and forth in a series of moves. Each move forms new shapes with the string. You can find a video tutorial on WilderCompanion.com and see a variety of other ways to play online. Here's some instructions to get you started.

What You Need

- about 60 inches (150 cm) of yarn tied in a loop

What to Do

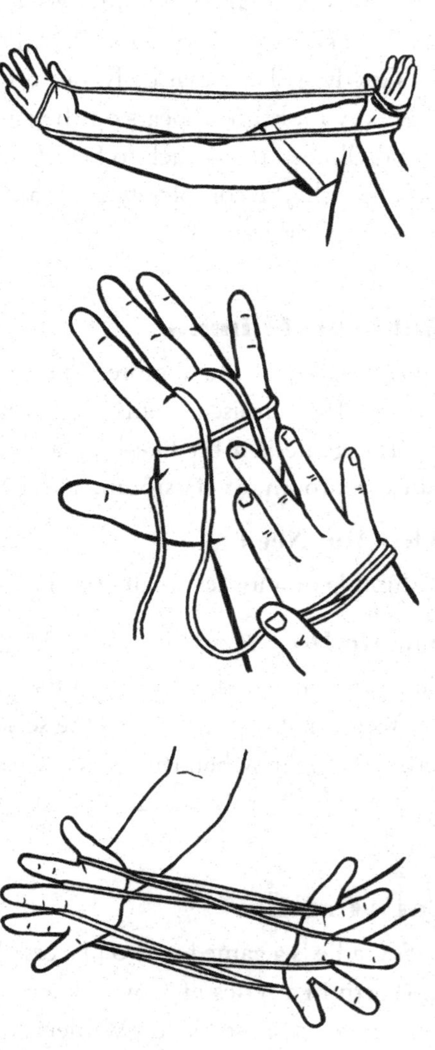

1. The first player begins by making a cat's cradle. He or she stretches the yarn loop around the back of both hands. The yarn rests between the pointer fingers and the thumbs on each hand.
2. The player then tucks each hand under the string to wrap each hand in string again.
3. Now, the player takes the middle finger of one hand and slides it under the string on the palm of the other hand, then spreads the hands apart. He or she then does the same on the opposite hand. This makes the cat's cradle shape, as shown.
4. Now you're ready to begin play. Get a parent's permission to go online to www.wildercompanion.com/2020/03/cats-cradle-tutorial.html to learn how to pass the cat's cradle from person to person and make new shapes.
5. Restart the game if the strings don't make a new shape.
6. (Optional) Play in a group by sitting in a circle. Pass the cat's cradle to the person sitting next to you and see if you can pass it all the way around the circle.
7. (Optional) With a parent's permission, you can do more research online about other shapes to make—there are a lot of fun and challenging ways to play cat's cradle!

Sweet Potato Garden

Mr. Edwards brought sweet potatoes for Christmas dinner. Ma set some aside to save for her garden. She probably planned to grow slips from the sweet potatoes. You can do the same.

Sweet potatoes are a tropical plant, but they grow in a variety of climates. They need about four months of growing time in warm soil. Sweet potatoes use a lot of space in gardens because the stem and leaves grow as a vine.

Grow your sweet potatoes from an organic sweet potato—or just one from a friend's garden. Grocery store sweet potatoes don't work well because they're often covered in wax.

What You Need

- sweet potato
- jar or glass cup
- toothpicks
- water
- sunny garden area

What to Do

1. Place the round end of a sweet potato in a jar in late March or early April. If the potato is too small to lodge in the mouth of the jar, push a few toothpicks into it to hold it up. Fill the jar with water, covering about half of the sweet potato. Place the jar in a sunny, warm window so the first leaves of the sweet potato plant, called slips, can grow. Refill the water as needed.
2. Stems and leaves will begin spouting out of the top of the sweet potato. These are called slips. When the slips are 4 inches (10 cm) or longer with leaves, carefully twist off each slip.
3. Place the slips in jars, glasses, or bowls. With the slips standing in their containers, fill each container about halfway with water. Be careful not to cover the leaves. Add fresh water daily to keep the slips healthy so they can grow roots. One sweet potato's slips can produce *a lot* of sweet potatoes. If you don't want to harvest a lot of them, share the slips with friends and family.
4. When the slips grow many roots, they are ready to plant in your garden. Do not plant them too early. Plan to plant the sweet potato slips about a month after the last frost. Days and nights need to be warm (possibly late May or early June). If you live in a cold climate with a short growing season, consider planting the slips in a container indoors.

5. Prepare your garden area by loosening the soil at least 12 inches deep (30 cm). Dig holes about 12 inches (30 cm) apart. The holes need to hold all the roots on the slip. If planting multiple rows of sweet potatoes, the rows should be 3 feet (1 m) apart.
6. Water the sweet potatoes when the soil is dry. The new sweet potatoes grow underground. Vines grow above ground. When the vines have yellowed in the fall, it is time to harvest. It is better to harvest them early than to allow frost to damage them.
7. Sweet potatoes fresh from the garden aren't ready to eat yet. Allow them to "cure" in a dry, shady place for about ten days before eating.
8. Store the sweet potatoes in a warm, dry place. Don't store them in a plastic bag or in the refrigerator.

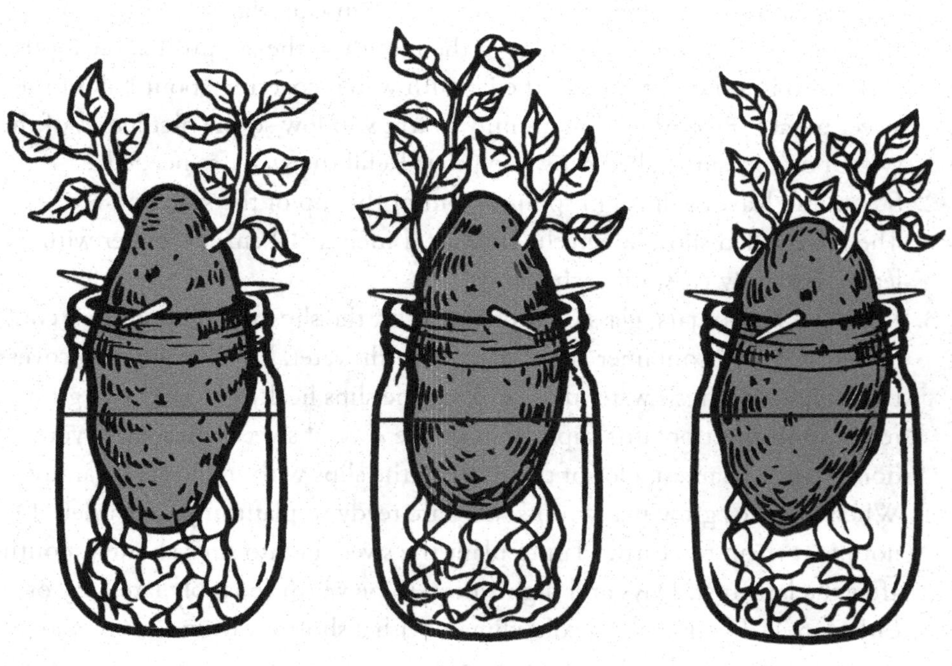

HOUSE TALK

- In the story, Pa made the quick decision to move. The family left all their furniture behind since it didn't fit in the wagon. If you had to move and could only take one small suitcase or backpack, what would you pack?
- Laura confronted Ma about her dislike of the American Indians. It took a lot of courage. What would you have said to Ma or a grown-up you know?
- When you see something you know is wrong, like racism, how can you take a stand?
- If you could only have a house 8 feet wide (2.4 m), what would you keep in it? Remember, the bathroom was still outdoors in the 1870s.
- What did Pa like about the land he chose for the house?
- Examine a door in your home. How is it similar and different than the door Pa made for his house?
- Laura desperately wanted to set Jack loose when the American Indians were in the house with Ma and Carrie. How would this help? How would it cause problems?
- Why do you think there isn't any mention of racism between Dr. Tan and the white settlers even though there was prejudice against the American Indians?
- When faced with the fear of the fire hurting Mary and Carrie, Laura had to help. Can you think of a time when you were afraid but brave?
- Mrs. Scott didn't seem to care that the land belonged to the American Indians. Do you think Pa thought the land should be the Indians' land or the settlers? What makes you think so?
- Pa didn't believe all the rumors he heard in Independence. When you hear a story and you're not sure if it's true, how can you know for sure?
- Earlier Pa said he thought the Osage neighbors were preparing for a hunt. Do you think he changed his mind? Why?
- Would you be excited to receive the Christmas gifts that Laura and Mary were given? Why were they so thankful?
- Pa didn't stop hunting the panther until he learned it was dead. Another man hunted it too. Why did they both search for it?
- What do you think was the biggest factor in Pa's change in attitude toward the American Indians by the end of the book? Was he right to feel this way?
- How would you feel if you had to move unexpectedly but didn't know where you were going to live?

Visitors tour this sod house built by the Laura Ingalls Wilder Museum in Walnut Grove, Minnesota. *Courtesy of Laura Ingalls Wilder Museum, Walnut Grove, Minnesota*

4

On the Banks of Plum Creek

WALNUT GROVE, MINNESOTA

The covered wagon took Pa, Ma, Mary, Laura, and Carrie away from Indian Territory through Missouri and Iowa. They finally arrived in Minnesota. Pa wanted to farm. He traded animals for the house and land. The family got quite the surprise when they learned the house was dug into a hillside and made of sod. They made the best of the situation, though, and even laughed when something unexpectedly came through the roof.

The Ingalls family lived about three miles from town. Mary and Laura walked to school each day. Eventually, the girls made friends at school, but Laura had a hard time getting along with one classmate.

Pa had big plans to farm the land. The harvest would mean a lot of money for the crops. But soon trouble arrived.

SOD HOUSES

When people wanted to build their first house on the prairie, they didn't typically use stones or logs to do it. The land was great for farming, but few trees grew there and few stores were available. So, many pioneers used what they could find to build homes: sod! Sod is the top layer of soil and the grass growing in it.

Many of the pioneer settlers made large, heavy bricks from layers of sod. One brick could weigh about 50 pounds (23 kg), and they were about 2 feet (60 cm) long. The bricks blended together and formed sturdy walls. But the houses' walls curved instead of being straight up and down. Like an igloo made of snow bricks, sod houses were a bit wider at the bottom so they could hold all the weight of the bricks. Building a house from sod bricks was difficult and time-consuming, but it didn't cost anything.

Some pioneer settlers used the prairie soil to build a different sort of house. Instead of only using sod bricks, they dug dirt out of the side of a hill and built some walls of sod bricks and added a roof into the hillside. This made a dugout house like the Ingallses' home on Plum Creek.

Often pioneers lived in a sod house or dugout for a short time. When they had time or enough money, they built a home from cut lumber.

A house from dirt was better than no house at all. And sod was a great insulator. Sod houses and dugouts were warm in the winter and cool in the summer. Plastered or wallpapered walls in the inside of the house could make it feel more like a regular house.

DIG DEEPER

Chapter 1

- Pa didn't go to the bank to take out a loan. Instead, Pa traded Pet and Patty for the house and land. Then Pa traded Bunny for the crops and oxen. Many pioneers helped one another by trading what they had instead of asking for a cash payment.
- The dugout surprised everyone, but Ma's reaction tells us she didn't like the idea of living in a sod house.
- Pete and Bright were oxen. Their strength made them a better choice than horses to plow and work the tough sod soil.

Chapter 4

- Pioneers didn't keep a lot of clothes. They didn't bother with bathing suits. Instead, they just wore old clothes.

Chapter 6

- Immigrants helped settle the Midwest like the rest of the United States. The Ingalls family moved so frequently they really did know people from many countries.

Chapter 8

- When Laura and Mary ruined Pa's straw stack, he was upset with them. After they explained they rolled down the stack instead of sliding, he turned away to hide his silent laughter.

Chapter 12

- Oxen were strong but slow. When the field work was done, Pa wanted horses again.

Chapter 13

- Mary J. Holmes wrote the classic novel *Millbank*.

Chapter 18

- A leech's bite is nearly painless because of numbing chemicals in its saliva. Doctors often used leeches to help sick people. Unfortunately, sometimes leeches made a sick person even sicker.

Chapter 20

- Laura and Mary ate the noon meal, called dinner, at school. (Like other families then, they called the evening meal supper.) All the other students lived close enough to go home to eat with their families.
- When the new church was built, the belfry sat without a bell. Though Pa's boots were in terrible shape, he gave his boot money for the bell. The Union Congregational Church was important to the family. Today, a private home in Walnut Grove, Minnesota, sits where the Ingallses' church used to be. However, Pa's bell still rings every Sunday in the local English Lutheran Church' bell tower.

Chapter 26

- Pa and Ma knew it would be hard to pay bills without money from the harvest. But it wasn't until the grasshoppers laid eggs that they really worried. With egg pods in nearly every inch of soil, they knew the grasshopper problem would only get worse. Since the family moved out of the dugout, they needed money to pay for the new house and some necessities. So Pa walked east to look for work. Other men did too. Some families gave up on their homesteading dream and returned east for good.

THE PLAGUE OF LOCUSTS

Just as Laura Ingalls Wilder described, insects arrived in a cloud and ate every plant in sight. They even ate curtains, clothing, and leather. Though described as grasshoppers in the book, scientists call them locusts. These insects were Rocky Mountain locusts (*Melanoplus spretus*).

Grasshoppers and locusts are very similar when in normal populations. When locusts become overcrowded, however, they develop long wings and migrate in huge swarms. These swarms can cause incredible damage. Grasshoppers do not swarm by the millions. And though grasshoppers eat plants, they won't eat entire crops over a large region.

Rocky Mountain locusts swarmed the Great Plains for centuries. They were part of the natural landscape. But they caused the most devasting damage from 1874 to 1877.

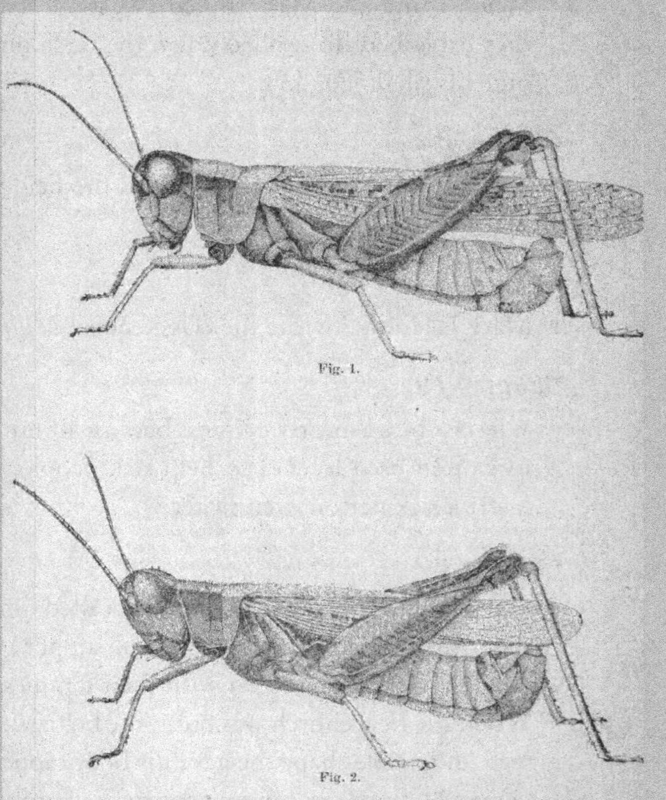

Rocky Mountain Locust (top) and Red-legged Grasshopper (bottom). The More Destructive Grasshoppers of Kansas, *University of Kansas, 1897*

Dr. A. L. Child estimated the swarm to be 1,800 miles (2,900 km) long and about 110 miles (180 km) wide in Nebraska in 1875. The swarm may have contained 3.5 trillion locusts! That's what Dr. Jeffrey Lockwood from the University of Wyoming estimated. Experts think they infested about 2 million square miles (5.2 million square km) of land and caused $200 million in crop damage, which would be about $116 billion today. They swarmed from the eastern Rocky Mountains to Iowa, and from Canada to Texas.

Surprisingly, the Rocky Mountain locust went extinct. The last recorded sighting was in 1902 in Canada. It's been over a hundred years since the last Rocky Mountain locust was last seen. Scientists generally agree the Rocky Mountain locust lost its habitat as settlers moved west. Settlers farmed the fertile river valleys of the Rockies to feed the gold and silver miners who swarmed into the area, which led to the locust's extinction.

Other species of locusts still torment people around the world and on every continent but Antarctica. However, no swarms compare in size to the Rocky Mountain locusts that devastated the American frontier.

Chapter 27

- Grass and other vegetation could not grow again without rain. But that wasn't the biggest problem—the creek and well dried up! Thankfully, a nearby spring dripped enough water to keep Ma and the girls alive.
- Ma read about the plague of locusts from the Bible. You can find that Bible story in Exodus, chapter 10.

Chapter 28

- When Pa finally wrote a letter, he sent news that he walked 300 miles (480 km) before he found work. The work was exhausting, but he earned a dollar for each day in the wheat fields.

Chapter 29

- You can read about Laura's doll, Charlotte, in *Little House in the Big Woods*. The new Charlotte looked different.

Chapter 32

- The grasshopper eggs hatched when spring arrived. The insects were tiny at first, but they grew quickly and shed their exoskeletons. They ate and ate. And they grew and grew before marching away.

Chapter 33

- Pa planted turnips because they grow in the late summer. The grasshoppers had eaten the other garden fruits and vegetables.
- Laura spotted a smoke cloud in the distance. Pa had plowed a firebreak before he left. With the overturned soil, the fire wouldn't have any fuel (like grass) to burn. Ma knew the fire would go out so she wasn't worried about their home. The firebreak worked! But the wind blew lots of dry tumbleweeds past the firebreak.

Chapter 35

- Out on the prairie, the only trees available were along the creek. Pa needed wood to heat the house, but he was careful to take only mature trees. Not only did he get more wood per tree, but he also saved the young trees for the future.

Chapter 37

- Ma and the girls played bean-porridge hot, a hand-clapping game, to pass the time while they missed Pa. You may be more familiar with the rhyme "Pease Porridge Hot." The songs have the same tune and similar words.

Chapter 40

- Some animals burrow into snow and make dens to hibernate through the winter. Just like a fluffy sleeping bag or coat keeps you warm, deep snow keeps the cold air away from a warm body. Snow acts as an insulator. And the body's heat keeps the air warm enough to survive.

WHERE IS PLUM CREEK

Laura Ingalls Wilder never mentioned the name of the town the Ingalls family lived in her book *On the Banks of Plum Creek*. However, records show the family lived in Walnut Grove, Minnesota, from 1874 to 1876, and from 1877 to 1879.

Garth Williams visited Laura and Almanzo Wilder at their home in Mansfield, Missouri in 1947 after he'd been hired to illustrate a new edition of the Little House books. Laura told Williams how to find the dugout site, though it was no longer there upon his arrival.

It wasn't until Garth Williams visited Walnut Grove that its residents learned their town was "Plum Creek." Today, Walnut Grove visitors can visit the site where the dugout used to be.

Plum Creek. *Courtesy of Laura Ingalls Wilder Museum, Walnut Grove, Minnesota*

LIVE LIKE LAURA

Corn Dodgers with Molasses

When Pa, Ma, and Carrie went to town, Laura and Mary had their noon dinner by themselves. They ate corn dodgers with molasses and drank milk.

Corn dodgers are a lot like johnnycakes but can be a finger food. Try them as a simple meal.

Adult supervision required.

What You Need

- 2 cups (480 mL) cornmeal
- 1½ teaspoons (7.5 mL) salt
- 1 tablespoon (15 mL) granulated sugar
- 1½ cups (360 mL) boiling water
- 2 tablespoons (30 mL) vegetable oil
- ¼ cup (60 mL) shortening

What to Do

1. Place cornmeal, salt, and sugar in a medium-sized bowl. Stir to mix well. Then have an adult pour the boiling water and the oil over the cornmeal mixture. Mix well.
2. When the mixture is cool enough to handle, divide the dough into four parts: divide into two halves and then divide those in half again. Shape each dough piece into a patty about ¾ inch (2 cm) thick. They can be round or oval.
3. Melt shortening in a nonstick frying pan or cast iron skillet over medium heat.
4. With an adult's help, place the corn cakes in the hot oil. Be careful to avoid spattering grease. Fry them until browned on the bottom. Then turn them over and brown the other side. Cook each side four to six minutes.
5. Carefully remove from the pan and drain on paper towels. Serve with molasses or maple syrup.

Dumplings and Gravy

Pa got a wild goose for Thanksgiving dinner. Since Ma didn't have an oven, she couldn't roast the goose. Instead, she cooked it in water to make a stew. She made it a special meal by adding dumplings to the goose stew.

Dumplings are almost like biscuits, but instead of being baked in the oven, they are cooked on top of meat and gravy or stew in a pot. You can try the dumplings over your favorite stew instead of the chicken or goose if you prefer.

Adult supervision required.

What You Need

- 2 cups (480 mL) chicken or goose, cooked and chopped
- 4 cups (960 mL) chicken broth (or water)
- 2 cups (480 mL) flour
- 4 teaspoons (20 mL) baking powder
- 1 teaspoon (5 mL) granulated sugar
- 1 teaspoon (5 mL) salt
- ¼ teaspoon (1 mL) pepper
- 1 cup (240 mL) milk

What to Do

1. Place meat in a large stock pot and cover with about 2 inches (5 cm) of chicken broth or water. The pot should be about ⅓ of the way full. Do not overfill.
2. With an adult's help, bring the pot to boil over medium heat.
3. In a medium sized bowl, mix together flour, baking powder, sugar, salt, and pepper.
4. Slowly add milk to the flour mixture and stir until a thick batter forms.
5. Scoop large tablespoons of dumpling dough and drop them on top of boiling mixture in a single layer around the pot.
6. Reduce heat to medium-low.
7. Place a lid on the pot. Cook dumplings covered for 10 minutes. Do not open the lid.
8. After 10 minutes remove the lid. Cook for 10 more minutes uncovered and serve.

Stewed Plums

For Thanksgiving dinner, Ma served goose, dumplings, mashed potatoes, corn dodgers, and gravy. Along with that, the family had butter, milk, and stewed dried plums. Dried plums are also called prunes. Stewed plums are sweet and healthy.

What You Need

- 1 cup (240 mL) prunes
- water

Adult supervision required.

What to Do

1. Place the prunes in a pot. Separate any prunes that are stuck together.
2. Cover them with water.
3. Have an adult bring the pot to a boil over high heat.
4. Once the water is boiling, reduce the heat to low. Cover and simmer for 20 minutes.
5. Serve, slightly cooled, in a bowl.

Star Garland

Ma showed Mary and Laura how to fold long strips of brown wrapping paper. Then they cut pieces of the folded paper, leaving a row of stars. Create your own star garland to hang.

What You Need

- long paper, any color (brown paper bag or wrapping paper)
- scissors
- pen or pencil

What to Do

1. Trim the paper to the width and length you want your garland to be.
2. Fold the paper back and forth, like an accordion. Make the length between folds as wide as you want each star in the garland to be.
3. Draw a large star on the front of the paper accordion. Two (or more) of the star's points must go off the paper on the two opposite edges where the accordion's folds are.

4. Holding the paper accordion together, cut through the layers of the accordion along the star's outline. Do not cut the tips of the stars that reach the folded edges.
5. Unfold your star garland to hang it.
6. (Optional) Try making a miniature star garland using smaller strips of paper for fun.

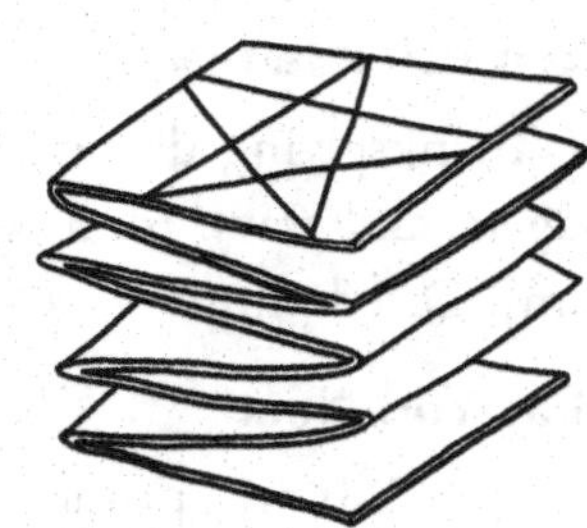

Vanity Cakes

Ma planned a country party complete with a special treat: vanity cakes. Made from fried dough, they puffed up and had a hollow center. Ma didn't sweeten her vanity cakes, but you can with a dusting of powdered sugar. These vanity cakes are similar to funnel cake.

You'll need a candy thermometer or instant thermometer to check the oil temperature.

Adult supervision required.

What You Need

- vegetable oil (enough to fill a pot with 2–3 inches [5–8 cm] of oil)
- 2 large eggs
- ¼ teaspoon (1 mL) salt
- 1 cup (240 mL) all-purpose flour, divided
- confectioner's sugar (optional, for dusting)

What to Do

1. With an adult, heat oil to 350°F (180°C) over medium (or medium-high) heat.

2. Whisk the egg and salt together for 1 minute. The egg mixture should be foamy.
3. Stir in ¼ cup (60 mL) of flour a little at a time. The batter should become stiff.
4. Place the rest of the flour on a plate or in a large, shallow bowl.
5. Pinch off a piece of dough about the size of a walnut. Flatten it to form a patty. Place the patty in the flour. Turn it over so the patty is completely covered in flour.
6. Have an adult drop one patty in the oil. Cook for about three minutes, turning every 30 seconds.
7. Use a slotted spoon to remove the cakes from the oil when lightly browned. Place them on a folded paper towel on a plate to drain. Sprinkle lightly with confectioner's sugar, if desired.
8. Cook the remaining vanity cakes a few at a time.
9. Allow to cool before serving.

Feed a Grasshopper

There were so many grasshoppers that the Ingalls family could hear them eating. You can hear one, too, if you listen closely.

First, catch a grasshopper. Gently hold it in your hand or place it in a jar with air holes. Grasshoppers eat most plants. Try feeding it grass or leaves from a tree. Can you hear it?

Grow Grass

After a drought, rain finally brought relief to the prairie. Grass grew! Laura noticed blades of grass poking through the soil the day after the rain. With sun and water, grass grows quickly. Find out how fast it grows.

What You Need

- disposable or recycled cup
- potting soil
- grass seed
- water

What to Do

1. Fill the cup most of the way with soil. Pat it down.
2. Sprinkle grass seed over the soil.
3. Water the grass. Place the cup in the sun.
4. Check the soil daily and note how much the grass has grown. If it is dry, lightly moisten it with water.

Popcorn String

The first time Mary and Laura saw a Christmas tree, it was decorated with gifts wrapped in colored paper, silk scarves, mittens, and even shoes! Strings of popcorn covered the tree. Decorate your own Christmas tree, doorway, or mantle with a popcorn string.

What You Need

- thread
- needle
- plain popcorn
- cranberries (optional)

What to Do

Thread the needle without cutting the thread from the spool. Then, poke the needle through a piece of popcorn and slide the popcorn down the thread. Continue to add popcorn until the string is the length you want it. To add a bit of color, add an occasional cranberry. The string needs to be *really* long to go around a tree many times. Really long thread tends to tangle, so be careful.

HOUSE TALK

- How did the family make the most of living in a dugout even though it wasn't what they expected?
- Why did Mary and Laura enjoy their days at the creek so much?
- When the family visited the swimming hole on a hot day, Laura disobeyed Pa and went into deep water. Pa pulled her underwater to teach her a lesson. Did it work?

- Ma told Laura it was easy to be naughty once you begin. Can you remember a time you did something wrong and didn't stop right away?
- Pa, Ma, and Carrie went to town. They left Laura and Mary home alone though they were young. That would not be OK today. What is the difference between now and then?
- The loose cattle ate the hay and scared Mary. How did she still show bravery?
- Laura explored the creek and found trouble when the snow thawed. Why didn't Ma scold Laura after she went to the footbridge?
- How was the new house Pa built different than the log cabin he built in *Little House on the Prairie*?
- Ma made curtains from old sheets. In what other ways did the Ingallses reuse fabric and old clothes?
- Laura helped Pa build and set the fish trap. Why do you think he stayed to watch the fish when he had work to do?
- Why did the family eat fish three times a day, for a long time, without complaining? Why didn't Pa just hunt like usual? (Think about the animal life cycle and what happens during the spring.)
- When Mary and Laura needed the slate pencil, why didn't they just take it like Mr. Oleson suggested and let Pa pay for it later?
- Why did Nellie Oleson go out of her way to invite Laura and Christy to her party?
- What do you think amazed Laura the most at Nellie's party?
- Laura carefully planned her revenge on Nellie. Who was crueler, Nellie or Laura? Why?
- Ma and the girls drank water from the spring when the well and creek dried up. How could the animals have gotten water?
- How did the rain give Ma and the girls hope?
- Compare Laura's newly fixed Charlotte doll to her description in *Little House in the Big Woods*. How did Charlotte change?
- Name several things that made the Christmas service at the church special.
- Why did Pa go east to look for work and not in a different direction?
- Ma appreciated good neighbors like Mr. Nelson. How can you be a good neighbor, even when there isn't a fire to fight?
- How did Pa surprise the family when he arrived home?
- Why did Ma leave the lamp in the window overnight when Pa went to town?
- Why was the family so happy without presents or candy at Christmas?

Charles Ingalls worked for the Chicago and North Western Railway as it extended the railroad to the town that would become De Smet, Dakota Territory. *Detroit Publishing Company, Library of Congress*

5

By the Shores of Silver Lake

DE SMET, DAKOTA TERRITORY

Aunt Docia arrived with an important invitation for Pa: Uncle Hi wanted Pa to be his bookkeeper and timekeeper. It was a railroad job that paid $50 a month. With his dreams of farming ruined by the grasshoppers, Pa couldn't pass up the offer.

So, the Ingalls family packed up again. This time they moved west to a temporary railroad camp in Dakota Territory. The workers prepared the ground for railroad tracks and a town that would come later.

While Pa worked for the railroad, the family lived in a shanty—a temporary house with just one room. The shanty belonged to the railroad. Where would the family stay when the railroad work finished? And would Pa ever find his homestead and file a claim?

THE HOMESTEAD ACT

President Abraham Lincoln signed the Homestead Act of 1862 into law. It encouraged people to move west by making land cheap and easy to buy. The Homestead Act was important because a lot of people moved to unsettled and unpopulated areas on the American frontier. It opened the land west of the Mississippi River for settlement.

To qualify for Homestead Act land, a person had to be 21 years old. Then they paid a small fee for their 160 acres of land called a homestead. The land owner had to improve their land by building a home and farming the land for at least five years. Then they would own the land.

Many people took advantage of the Homestead Act, including former slaves, new immigrants wanting to become citizens, and women. Settlers claimed more than 270 million acres of land before the Homestead Act was repealed in 1976. People appreciated that it helped those who weren't rich buy land.

But homesteading was difficult. Crops often failed because of the dry climate on the prairie. Even experienced farmers couldn't win against nature. Many homesteaders weren't successful despite their hard work.

BETWEEN BOOKS

In real life, Charles and Caroline Ingalls had another child toward the end of their time in Walnut Grove, Minnesota. His name was Charles Frederick Ingalls. They called him Freddy.

When the Ingalls family left Walnut Grove, they first moved to Burr Oak, Iowa. Freddy died on August 27, 1876, before they reached Burr Oak. He was nine months old.

In Burr Oak, Charles and Caroline helped run the Masters Hotel. Even the girls worked there. This was a period Laura Ingalls Wilder left out of her books; she picked the story back up as Pa took the job offer in Dakota Territory.

Mary and Laura served meals at the Masters Hotel in Burr Oak, Iowa. *Courtesy of Laura Ingalls Wilder Park & Museum, Burr Oak, Iowa*

FACT OR FICTION?

In the opening chapter, the family was healing from scarlet fever. Ma was still weak, but Mary suffered the most. She lost her eyesight.

Laura Ingalls Wilder's books are based on her childhood on the American frontier, but she included some fictional elements. Did she make up Mary's blindness?

Research proves Mary did go blind in 1879 when she was fourteen years old. But did scarlet fever cause the infection? In 2013, a pediatrician shared her research about Mary and scarlet fever in an article.

Dr. Beth A. Tarini and her team read Laura Ingalls Wilder's memoir, *Pioneer Girl*. They found newspaper articles about Mary's illness. They even studied medical journals from the 1800s and compared them to information today about blindness and infections.

Evidence points to an infection and swelling of Mary's brain. Dr. Tarini thinks viral meningoencephalitis may have caused Mary's loss of sight instead of scarlet fever.

So what made Laura Ingalls Wilder write about scarlet fever? Mary's illness was generally described as "brain fever," which includes a lot of illnesses, including scarlet fever. Wilder didn't remember the actual name for Mary's illness. It's also possible that she or her editors wanted to use an illness that was familiar to readers. Books like *Little Women* mentioned scarlet fever, so it would be better known.

DIG DEEPER

Chapter 3

- Ma and the girls traveled about 10 miles (16 km) by train to Tracy, Minnesota.

THE RAILROAD

Trains moved people and goods. At first, most railroads in America were concentrated on the East Coast, but soon they spread west. Settlers arrived on the new railroads. Trains and the Homestead Act helped people settle the land in the West.

Trains were much faster than wagons. They were designed to carry heavy loads too. A loaded covered wagon might travel just 10–20 miles (16–32 km) a day depending on the weather and land. But a train could travel 20 miles (30 km) an hour. That sounds slow by today's standards, but in those days it radically changed transportation.

After settlers arrived in the West, the railroads connected them to friends and family back East. Trains brought the mail and must-have items like groceries, tools, fabrics, and more. Railroads were even important to agriculture. Cowboys and farmers loaded cattle into railroad cars and shipped them to distant towns.

Chapter 4

- Hotels served as restaurants for travelers. They were usually very close to train stations.

Chapter 6

- Aunt Docia was too busy to do laundry, so she paid someone to do it for her. She cooked for nearly 50 men without the conveniences of premade food, a microwave, or a dishwasher. Scrubbing clothes on a washboard, drying them on the clothesline, and ironing the dry laundry took a long time. Many people did laundry over a two-day period. Aunt Docia just didn't have time for that.
- Laura was shocked at the idea of a 13-year-old getting married. She wanted to forget about growing up. Couples typically married at a younger age in the 1800s than they do today, but 13 was startlingly young.

Chapter 7

- Read more about Uncle Henry and Cousin Charley in *Little House in the Big Woods.*
- Homesteaders and railroad workers needed to build homes quickly. Little shanties, typically with just one room and a low sloped roof, provided a hasty home and shelter. But they didn't have insulation. Sometimes the shanties even had large cracks between the boards, so they didn't really keep out the cold winter weather—even with a warm stove. Many homesteaders built an addition onto their shanties and added insulation when they were able.

Chapter 8

- A slough is wet, swampy land. The word *slough* (as defined here) rhymes with *flew.*
- Silver Lake isn't much of a lake today. It's mostly a slough.
- The center of a drop-leaf table always looks like a table, but the sides (or

A drop-leaf table saved a lot of space in small rooms.
Metropolitan Museum of Art, Wikimedia Commons

leaves) of the table can be folded down on a hinge. During mealtimes, the leaves prop up and lay flat to extend the table surface. The leaves make the table much larger.

- Big Jerry was a man of two races, Caucasian and American Indian, so many people described him as a "half-breed." Today is an offensive description that should never be used.
- Ma remembered her fear of American Indians from the time they lived in Indian Territory. Pa reminded Ma of Big Jerry's good qualities, though. Soon Ma helped Big Jerry care for Old Johnny.

Chapter 12

- Some swans really do measure as large as 8 feet (2.4 m) from wing tip to wing tip. That's as wide as a couch! The wingspan is measured from the longest feather on one wing to the longest feather on the other wing when both are spread.

Chapter 13

- Where would the Ingallses live? The railroad built—and owned—the family's shanty. With the railroad workers gone, Pa's job was over. The railroad company would take down shanties and move the lumber to the next railroad camp to build shanties there. The Ingallses couldn't live in the shanty anymore. Even if they could, they didn't have any fuel, such as logs or coal, to warm their home. The shanty had thin walls and no insulation. The family planned to go east for the winter until Pa came home with hopeful news.
- Mr. Boast went to Pa for help. Mr. Boast sold some animals to a man, but the man never finished paying for them. With no law enforcement close by, Pa wrote a fake but official-looking paper called a writ of attachment to scare the man into giving back the animals. This document helped the man pretending to be a sheriff take back the team. The man who hadn't paid knew he'd done wrong, but he didn't realize that there wasn't a real court or sheriff nearby to enforce the law.

Chapter 14

- Ma celebrated living in a real house—not just a shanty—with soda crackers and canned peaches. They may not have had a store nearby, but the surveyors' pantry was stocked. Learn how to make soda crackers on page 86.

Chapter 15

- A man was sick with consumption. Like many others, he thought the prairie climate would help him. Today this deadly disease is known as tuberculosis, a dangerous lung infection. Tuberculosis was once the deadliest disease in the United States, but today doctors treat it with antibiotics.

Visitors tour the original surveyors' house where the Ingalls family lived during the long winter. *Photo © Laura Ingalls Wilder Memorial Society, De Smet, South Dakota*

Chapter 16

- With no people nearby (and no electronics), the Ingalls family made their own entertainment. Ma and the girls spent winter days sewing, crocheting, and knitting. Pa made a game of checkers, though he didn't play it often. Learn how to make your own checkerboard on page 88.

Chapter 18

- Wolves hunt animals, but they rarely hurt people. Pa saw the tracks of two buffalo wolves, which are in the same family as gray wolves (*Canis lupus* species).

Chapter 19

- Think about how the family delighted in making gifts for one another. Without a store nearby, the Ingalls family relied upon their own skills. Even the children made thoughtful, useful presents to give.

Chapter 22

- Imagine hosting a party in a small bedroom with a dirt floor for eight people. Remember to leave room for the table and stove. You might not have much room to move around. The Boasts and Ingallses celebrated the beginning of 1880 in a small space too.
- Ma appreciated the stories in Mrs. Boast's newspapers. She even told Laura to skip the work to read aloud. Ma called the story a "continued story." It can

also be called a serial story. Often writers would sell their stories to monthly or weekly newspapers and magazines. Books by Charles Dickens, Wilkie Collins, and Harriet Beecher Stowe were all first published like this.

Chapter 23

- The town's name would be De Smet, located in the Dakota Territory. In 1889 the Dakota Territory became the states of North Dakota and South Dakota.

CHURCH CHANGES

The very first church meeting in De Smet was in the Ingallses' home. They met on February 29, 1880. The Ingallses were founding members of the De Smet Congregational Church. Later, the De Smet Congregational Church met in the train depot until they had a building of their own. Charles Ingalls helped build the actual church building in 1882.

In 1967 the De Smet Congregational Church moved to a new building. The church Charles helped build is now called the De Smet Alliance Church.

Chapter 24

- Ma charged each person she served 25¢ for a meal. For another 25¢ per person (or horse), they could spend the night. Ma wasn't trying to get rich. Some would say her fee barely covered the inconvenience of cooking, cleaning, and hosting strangers.

Chapter 26

- Before Pa finished building his store in town, the family moved into it knowing they couldn't stay at the surveyors' house much longer. It was the family's first experience living in town.

Chapter 27

- The Ingallses didn't live in town long. Pa hurried to leave after someone was killed nearby. They were all happy to move once Pa built the shanty. Each family member had different reasons for wanting to be on the homestead.

Chapter 29

- Out on the prairie, trees only grew near water sources like lakes. Pa dug up some cottonwood trees and planted them around their house. The house no longer stands, but today De Smet visitors can see five cottonwoods on the land where the family lived.

LIVE LIKE LAURA

See for Mary

When Mary lost her eyesight, Laura became Mary's "eyes." Laura described the things she saw to Mary in detail so her sister could better understand her world. Mary imagined the things she could not see. If you know someone who is blind, ask them what kind of descriptions or information is the most helpful to help them know their environment.

Can you "see" for a friend? Take your friend to a new place. It might be a park, garden, or even a room. While your friend keeps his or her eyes closed, describe what you see. Use as many details as possible to help your friend really understand what is there.

Dried Apples

Ma used dried apples to make treats like applesauce and apple pie during the long winter months when fresh fruit wasn't available. With a bit of water, the dried fruit could be used in recipes just like regular fruit. Baking apple slices at a low temperature removes the moisture from them.

Dried apples make a great snack. Or cook them with a bit of water to make dried applesauce.

Adult supervision required.

Note: This recipe requires the oven to be on for at least ten hours. Do not leave the oven unattended while it is on. You can keep the oven door closed and turn it off if you need to leave your home or go to bed.

What You Need

- 3 apples
- 4 cups (960 mL) cold water
- ½ cup (120 mL) lemon juice
- 2 tablespoons (30 mL) granulated sugar (optional)
- 1 tablespoon (15 mL) cinnamon (optional)

What to Do

1. Wash and core the apples. Peeling them is optional.

2. With an adult's help, slice the apples thinly. A mandoline works well for this, but you can also use a paring knife.
3. Place the apple slices in a bowl with the water and lemon juice for 10–20 minutes. This prevents browning.
4. Have an adult preheat the oven to 200°F (95°C).
5. Spray cooling racks (or cookie sheets) lightly with cooking spray. Arrange the apple slices in a single layer on the racks or cookie sheets. The apples can touch but should not overlap.

6. To make the optional cinnamon mixture, mix the sugar and cinnamon in a small bowl and lightly sprinkle over the apple slices.
7. Bake at 200°F (95°C) for 10–12 hours.
8. Remove the tray from the oven. Try to bend an apple slice. If it bends, the apples need more baking time. If the apple snaps and cracks when bent, it is done. When apples are done, keep the apple slices in the oven and keep the door closed. Turn off the oven. Leave the apples in the oven overnight for extra drying time.
9. Remove the dried apples from the oven and place them in an airtight container.
10. Snack on apple "chips" or mix them with granola or trail mix. You can also cook dried apples with water until they are soft. Then drain the apples and mash them with a fork to make applesauce.

Soda Crackers

Ma celebrated living in a real house instead of a shanty with soda crackers and canned peaches. Soda crackers might look like saltines but they're soft. The butter and salt give them a delicious taste.

There are a lot of steps, but the crackers are simple enough for you to make with only a little help from an adult.

Adult supervision required.

Note: You won't bake and eat the crackers the same day you make the dough. It rests in the refrigerator overnight.

What You Need

- ¾ cup (180 mL) all-purpose flour
- 1 teaspoon (5 mL) instant or bread yeast
- ⅛ teaspoon (0.5 mL) baking soda
- ⅛ teaspoon (0.5 mL) cream of tartar
- ⅛ teaspoon (0.5 mL) salt
- ½ teaspoon (2.5 mL) granulated sugar
- ⅓ cup (60 mL) warm water
- 1 tablespoon (15 mL) shortening
- salt (sea salt or pretzel salt works best)
- 1 tablespoon (15 mL) butter, melted

What to Do

1. Stir ½ cup (120 mL) flour (not all of it), yeast, baking soda, cream of tartar, salt, and sugar in a mixing bowl. Stir well. Mix in the warm water and shortening until combined.
2. Now mix in ¼ cup (60 mL) flour to make a drier dough you can knead.
3. Lightly flour a clean counter. Knead the dough on the floured surface for 3–5 minutes, then shape it into a ball.
4. Lightly oil the inside of a medium or large bowl. Place the dough in the bowl and then flip the dough over so all sides of the dough ball are coated with oil. Cover the bowl tightly with plastic wrap and place in the refrigerator overnight.

5. Remove the soda cracker dough from the refrigerator and have an adult preheat the oven to 425°F (220°C). Lightly grease a large cookie sheet or line it with parchment paper.
6. Lightly flour a clean work surface. Deflate the dough by gently punching it once. Then place it on the floured work area. Let the dough rest for 5 minutes.
7. If you are not experienced using a rolling pin, you may want to ask an adult for help. On the floured surface, use a floured rolling pin to roll the dough into a very thin rectangle. It should be about 1⁄16 inch (0.16 cm) thin (a ruler helps!). That's really thin.
8. Fold the dough into three equal segments like you are folding a piece of paper to put it in an envelope: take one end and fold it about two-thirds of the way across. Then take the other end and place it on top of the end you just folded, creating three layers of dough.
9. Fold the three layers of dough in half, perpendicular to the folds you just made.
10. Pick up the dough and add another dusting of flour below it. Roll the dough out again, making sure it is 1⁄16 inch thick. If it doesn't want to stretch, let it rest for five minutes and then try again. You want it to be as thin as possible.
11. Transfer the dough to the prepared cookie sheet.
12. Use a fork to create lots of pinpricks all over the dough.
13. Cut the dough into squares. A pizza cutter or sharp knife works well.
14. Separate the dough squares slightly. The soda crackers should be close together but not touching.
15. Lightly sprinkle the cracker dough with salt.
16. Bake the crackers for 10–15 minutes. They should be lightly browned.
17. After removing the crackers from the oven, brush melted butter on them. Transfer the crackers to a cooling rack. When completely cooled, store the soda crackers in an airtight container.

Homemade Checkerboard

To pass the quiet winter days, Pa made a checkerboard for the family. Pa made his from wood, but you can weave one using construction paper. Use buttons or candy in two colors for your checkers.

What You Need

- 2 pieces construction paper, in contrasting colors, 10 inches by 8 inches (25 cm by 20 cm)
- pen or pencil
- ruler
- scissors
- glue

What to Do

1. Choose a paper color to be the background of your checkerboard. The other paper color will be cut and woven into it.
2. Fold the background paper in half.
3. Keep the background paper folded. Use a ruler to draw a line 1 inch (2.5 cm) from the open edge. You will not cut this line; it is a guide to know when to stop cutting (see gray line in illustration).
4. Next you'll draw lines 1 inch (2.5 cm) apart connecting the folded edge to the line you drew in Step 3. Make seven lines total.
5. Keep the paper folded. Cut the seven marked lines beginning at the fold. Stop each cut at the first line you drew in Step 3.
6. Unfold the paper and lay it flat.
7. Cut eight strips from the contrasting paper. Each should be about 1 inch (2.5 cm) thick.

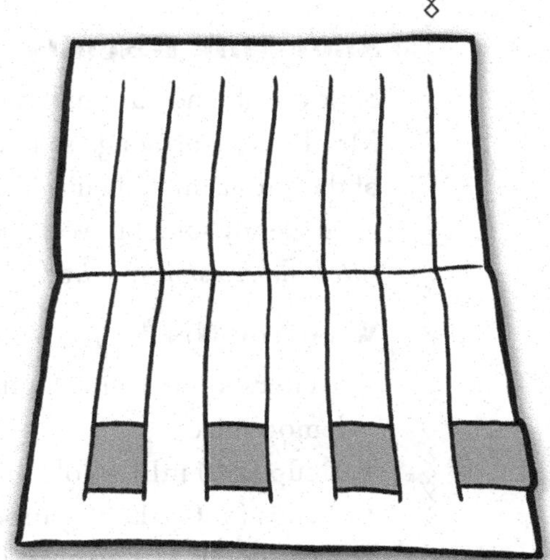

8. Weave one strip through the background paper, along one edge of the cuts. Go over and under the paper slits in an alternating pattern.
9. Take another strip of paper and weave it through the slits, right next to where you wove the first one. Weave it to be the opposite of the first woven strip, going under and then over in a pattern.
10. Continue weaving in an alternate pattern until you have woven all eight strips of paper. Trim the paper strips to the length of the checkerboard. Glue down any loose paper strips.
11. Turn the weaving over. Glue down any loose paper strips on that side. Let the glue dry, then flip the weaving back over.
12. Use two colors of buttons or candy as your checker pieces. Get a partner and play!

Night Hike

Laura got antsy, so she and Carrie ventured out to the frozen Silver Lake. The moon shone brightly, lighting their path.

Take your own moonlit walk. Go outdoors at night with a friend, sibling, or adult, where there aren't any streetlights or headlights. It might be your backyard or a local park. Once you get near your destination, put your flashlights in your pockets. It may take a few minutes for your eyes to adjust, but soon you'll be able to see in the darkness. Listen to the night sounds and then cup your ears with your hands to see if you can hear even more interesting sounds. Use your senses to explore during your night hike.

Sour-Milk Biscuits

Sour dough and sour milk both make a light and fluffy biscuit. As Ma described to Mrs. Boast, sour-dough starter takes several days to make. But you can whip up a batch of these sour-milk biscuits in a just a few minutes. Ma would have used milk that had gone slightly sour, but you can make a substitute by adding a bit of vinegar to milk. *Adult supervision required.*

What You Need

- 1 tablespoon (15 mL) vinegar or lemon juice
- 1 cup (240 mL) whole milk
- 2 cups (480 mL) all-purpose flour
- 2 teaspoons (10 mL) baking powder
- 1 teaspoon (5 mL) salt
- ¼ teaspoon (1 mL) baking soda
- ½ cup (120 mL) butter, cold and cut into small slices

What to Do

1. Have an adult preheat the oven to 425°F (220°C).
2. Place 1 tablespoon (15 mL) vinegar or lemon juice in a liquid measuring cup. Add enough milk to make 1 cup (240 mL). Stir and set aside for 5 minutes. (The vinegar sours the milk and makes a buttermilk substitute.)
3. Grease a baking sheet with shortening or line it with parchment paper. Set it aside.
4. Stir together flour, baking powder, salt, and baking soda in a large bowl.
5. Using a large fork or pastry blender, mix in the butter. After several minutes, the mixture should look like a lot of pea-sized clumps of flour.
6. Make a well in the center of the flour mixture. Measure ¾ cup (180 mL) sour milk. Slowly stir it into the flour mixture. (Save the remaining milk for later.) Stir until the dough is wet, but do not overmix it.
7. Lightly flour a clean work surface, like a counter. Place the dough on the floured surface and pat the dough to form a rectangle using floured hands.
8. Fold the dough rectangle into thirds like you would a piece of paper before placing it in an envelope.
9. Use your hands to flatten and widen the folded dough into a larger rectangle. Then fold it into thirds again. Repeat once more, pressing and folding three times total.

10. Lightly flour your work surface again. Using your hands or a floured rolling pin, spread or roll the dough about ½ inch (1 cm) thick.
11. Use a floured biscuit cutter or a floured drinking glass (upside down) to cut out round biscuits. Place the cutter on the dough and press straight down. Do not press from side-to-side, or your biscuits won't rise evenly.
12. Transfer the cut biscuit dough to the prepared baking sheet. Place the biscuits about ½ inch (1 cm) apart. Brush the tops of the biscuits with the leftover sour milk. Rework the leftover dough to form more biscuits using the same process.
13. Bake for 13–15 minutes. The biscuits will be lightly browned when done. Serve warm with butter, gravy, or one of the other toppings described below.

Hot Biscuits with Honey or Applesauce

On Christmas morning, the Ingallses enjoyed hot biscuits with applesauce. The next week Mrs. Boast hosted New Year's dinner. She served hot biscuits with honey.

Make a batch of biscuits using the activity above or your favorite recipe and try them topped with honey and applesauce. Which topping do you prefer?

Sage and Onion Stuffing

When Pa spotted a flock of geese, Laura and Mary planned dinner. Mary wanted sage stuffing with a roast goose dinner. Laura wanted the stuffing flavored with onion instead. The girls bickered about it, but neither got what they wanted. This recipe includes both sage *and* onion as flavorings.
Adult supervision required.

What You Need

- ½ pound (0.2 kg) ground sausage (optional)
- ½ cup (120 mL) butter
- 1 cup (240 mL) finely chopped celery
- 1 cup (240 mL) finely chopped onion
- 4 cups (960 mL) chicken broth (or water)

- 2 teaspoons (10 mL) sage
- 1 bag seasoned croutons (about 12 ounces [340 g])

What to Do

1. Preheat the oven to 375°F (190°C).
2. If using sausage, form it into a large, thin patty. Place this in a frying pan. Over medium heat, brown both sides of the patty. Then crumble the meat. Set the meat aside.
3. Melt the butter in a medium saucepan, then add the celery and onion. Add chicken broth (or water). Cook for 7 minutes over medium heat.
4. Pour the broth mixture into a large bowl. Work carefully because the mixture will be hot. Stir in the sausage and sage. Gently stir in croutons. Add more broth or water if the mixture seems dry.
5. Place the mixture in a buttered or sprayed casserole dish. Cover it with aluminum foil. Bake at 375°F (190°C) for 20 minutes, then remove the foil and bake for 5 more minutes.

HOUSE TALK

- Why didn't Ma want to go to Dakota Territory? Why did Pa want to go? What would you want if you were part of the Ingalls family?
- Why do you think the meal at the hotel was so uncomfortable for Ma and the girls? How would it be different today?
- Ma and Mary didn't understand Laura's fascination with the railroad. What do you think Laura found so interesting?
- When payday came and the railroad workers were upset, how was Big Jerry helpful?
- Laura desperately wanted to help Pa when she knew the men were angry. Would she have been able to help?
- Since the railroad company didn't pay Uncle Hi the wages he earned, Aunt Docia and Lena took three wagons of supplies with them when they left as payment. Ma thought it was stealing. Pa said it was not. Who do you agree with?

- Ma and the girls spent their winter days sewing, crocheting, and knitting. Pa made a checkerboard. Why did Pa think checkers was a selfish game?
- When Laura saw the wolf, why didn't she tell Carrie about it?
- Pa finally found his perfect homestead. What did he like about it?
- Grace received a lot of attention for her new coat. Why do you think her sisters weren't jealous of her?
- Why didn't the family have a Christmas tree?
- The family sang many Christmas songs and hymns together. How do you think they knew the song lyrics?
- The house was full of secret gifts, but they needed more! Mr. and Mrs. Boast surprised the family on Christmas Eve with a visit. Mary was horrified at the idea of receiving any gifts when there weren't any for Mr. and Mrs. Boast. What would you do?
- The Ingallses had moved many times already. Do you think this would be their last move, like Ma said?
- Reverend Alden and Reverend Stuart brought hope during their surprise visit. The Ingallses learned of a college for blind people like Mary. How did Laura feel during their prayer meeting?
- The family was overwhelmed by a large number of travelling strangers. Why did they keep letting travelers stay?

Carrie, Mary, and Laura Ingalls posed for this picture shortly after moving to De Smet, South Dakota. *Photo © Laura Ingalls Wilder Memorial Society, De Smet, South Dakota*

6

The Long Winter

DE SMET, DAKOTA TERRITORY

The muskrat house gave Pa the first clue that the upcoming winter might be hard. Soon, an October blizzard lasted for three days. Then an American Indian warned a crowd in Harthorn's store that there would be seven months of blizzards. Pa's worries grew.

Pa knew his claim shanty couldn't keep out cold weather, let alone a brutal winter. So the family moved into Pa's empty store in town. It would be warmer than the claim shanty.

Soon they knew they were in trouble. The trains couldn't get through with supplies. The stores of De Smet sold all the food and fuel. Soon, the Ingalls family wondered if they would survive the terrible winter.

Two heroes risked everything to save the people of De Smet. Would the young men return?

FACT OR FICTION?

Laura Ingalls Wilder fictionalized (made up) parts of the Little House series. You may wonder if she exaggerated the story of the hard winter of 1880–1881. Meteorologist Barbara Mayes Boustead examined *The Long Winter*. She compared the book to weather and history records. Wilder's memory was surprisingly accurate, despite the many years that passed before she wrote the story. She remembered the length of blizzards as well as days of calm between storms. The last freight train really did stop in De Smet in late December.

There were no official weather records for De Smet in Dakota Territory for 1880–1881. However, other cities in the region received between 121 and 154 inches (335 and 427 cm) of snow that winter. That's more than 10 feet (300 cm) of snow throughout the winter—the snow drifts would have been even deeper! Records for the coldest temperatures in the area were also set that winter. Some of those records still stand today.

Laura Ingalls Wilder shared the true story of De Smet and her family in this tale of the long, hard winter. Though she fictionalized some parts of the book to improve the story, she did not exaggerate the brutal winter.

Deep snow surrounds a train engine in South Dakota in the 1800s.
South Dakota State Historical Society, South Dakota Archives

DIG DEEPER

Chapter 1

- Laura was used to working hard at home, and she wanted to make Pa's work easier. Ma didn't like the idea of Laura working in the field but knew Pa needed the help.

Chapter 4

- Ice formed on the quilt and frost on the nails during the October blizzard. The inside of the shanty had to be below freezing, 32 degrees Fahrenheit (0°C). Many people let the fire go out at night since they could stay warm in bed, but that makes a cold house! Find out the temperature of your home during the winter. If your home is heated, try to imagine how cold it would be if your only way to warm it was a fire or oven.

Chapter 6

- When the late fall weather is warm and dry after cold weather or a frost, it's often called an Indian summer. Since the origins of the term are unknown, we don't know whether the term was born out of prejudice against American Indians or not. It may have been, so it's best to avoid saying it. Today we can just call warm fall weather a second summer.
- Ma told the girls to go outside and get sunshine while they could. Sunshine provides vitamin D for our bodies. It's important for our bones and is good for us.

Chapter 7

- You can read about Royal and Almanzo Wilder's childhoods in Laura Ingalls Wilder's second book called *Farmer Boy*.
- Pa trusted his American Indian neighbor and moved the family to town right away. Think about whether you would believe a warning about seven months of blizzards. That would be a *long* winter.

Chapter 9

- Many pioneer children had to complete chores around the house or barn before going to school. Consider how you can help your family each day.
- In the 1800s (and well into the 1900s), teachers read and taught from the Bible even in public schools.
- Miss Garland didn't realize the storm was a blizzard. Laura recognized that the

winds were coming from all directions, which was one characteristic of a prairie blizzard.

Chapter 11

- The citizens of De Smet knew if they pitched in and helped shovel out the train, it could arrive sooner. It's also likely they read advertisements from the railroad. They would pay workers to shovel. The book said the men traveled 50 miles (80 km) to help clear the train tracks. Volga wasn't quite that far away, but it was still intense work.
- During this visit, Mr. Edwards gave Mary a gift of $20. Today that would be worth about $500! Mr. Edwards also delivered gifts from Santa Claus in *On the Banks of Plum Creek*. Though Mr. Edwards was an important character in the Little House books, some researchers think he is likely a fictional character based on a real person (or people). Others think Mr. Edwards represented a neighbor from Independence, Kansas, named Edmund Mason.

A handcar on rails.
Jules-Ernest Livernois, Wikimedia Commons

Chapter 12

- Flatirons remove wrinkles from clothing, but they had another use. People heated a flatiron and then put it under bed covers to warm up the bed.

Chapter 17

- Farmers and gardeners kept seeds from a good harvest to plant the next spring. It saved money and provided good seeds for the next year's crop.

HUNGRY OR STARVING?

There's a difference between starving and being hungry. Starvation happens when a person continually doesn't get the nutrition they need, even if they are eating. Starvation makes people grumpy and tired. They have trouble concentrating. It can lead to sunken eyes. The skin becomes pale. Muscles become smaller and weaker. Think about these symptoms as you read how people looked and acted in *The Long Winter*.

Many De Smet settlers arrived with a stock of needed supplies like food during the spring of 1880. The Ingalls family arrived the year before. They didn't bring food and only raised a small crop. Others in town may not have had a lot of food, but most likely had more than the Ingalls family.

Chapter 18

- The girls didn't expect gifts, so they didn't hang stockings at Christmas. Laura didn't hope for gifts of her own, but she found gifts to share with her family.

Chapter 19

- With no meat, coal, or kerosene in town, the family needed to save as much as possible. So they ate just two small meals each day. Ma didn't even wash the dishes after supper. Instead everyone went straight to bed to stay warm under the blankets after the fire went out. Using less fire saved fuel. Going to bed early also saved the button lamp's grease.

Chapter 25

- Census records from 1880 show 116 people lived in De Smet. According to the story, Almanzo risked his life to help the starving people of the town. He knew his wheat couldn't help that many people for months.

Chapter 27

- Almanzo Wilder and Cap Garland took the chance on what many thought was a wild goose chase. They didn't know if there was any wheat to find or if it was just a rumor. They didn't know where to find it. And even if they did find the wheat, a blizzard could kill them.

Chapter 29

- Cap and Almanzo didn't want to be paid for the wheat trip, they only wanted to help their neighbors. Mr. Loftus was a store owner, and he needed to make a profit from the items he sold. That's how businesses work. The people of De Smet didn't think it was right for him to take advantage of their desperation and make a *huge* profit. Mr. Loftus surprised them all in the end.

COLD WEATHER RISKS

Did you know your skin can freeze? It's called frostbite. You can get it if your skin is exposed to cold temperatures for a long time. You can even get frostbite if you're in extremely cold temperatures for just a few minutes.

Frostbite begins with the loss of color and all feeling in the skin. If it continues too long, the skin freezes. Then the ice in the skin blocks the blood flow. Doctors now know frostbitten skin must be warmed slowly and should never be rubbed—not even with snow.

Another risk of spending time outdoors in extreme cold is hypothermia. That's when the body's temperature gets too low. Symptoms of hypothermia are uncontrollable shivering, sleepiness, exhaustion, and unclear thinking. It's life-threatening.

Our bodies have a natural ability to create heat and keep a regular body temperature. But eventually if the body cannot stay warm, blood stays closer to vital organs like the heart, lungs, kidneys, and brain. That's why toes, fingers, ears, and noses are at the most risk for frostbite.

Prevent hypothermia and frostbite by moving blood through your limbs in cold temperatures. You can do this by running and swinging your arms. Seek medical attention immediately for frostbite and hypothermia.

Chapter 32

- Ma invited the Boasts for a special celebration dinner. It would be two days after getting her Christmas barrel. Ma needed that time to thaw the turkey.

Chapter 33

- After the Christmas feast in May, the Ingallses and Boasts continued to celebrate with singing. The different singing voices called tenor, alto, contralto, soprano, and bass accompanied Pa's fiddle. Listen to different singing voices online to hear the variety. Can you tell the difference?
- Desperate pioneers had to wait until May for the trains, long after the snow melted. The ground was too muddy to travel by wagon. Melting snow flooded rivers and creeks. Some railroad bridges washed out in the spring of 1881. So even when the snow melted off the train tracks, bridges still had to be repaired for the trains to travel west. It was a long wait.

FACT OR FICTION?

One surprising truth of Laura Ingalls Wilder's long winter is that her family did not live by themselves. A man, his wife, and their baby lived with the family.

The Masters family made that difficult winter even harder for the Ingallses. Even with so much work to be done just to grind wheat for the daily bread and twist hay for fuel, the Masterses, as boarders, did not help with the work, though they ate their share of the food.

LIVE LIKE LAURA

Ginger Water

Ma sent Carrie to the field with a refreshing drink for Laura and Pa. Ma made ginger water with vinegar, sugar, and ginger. This kept them hydrated while they worked. It also provided carbohydrates and nutrients they lost through their sweat. Some people call ginger water "switchel."

Just like sports drinks today, this is not an everyday drink. It's best to drink ginger water after working hard on a hot day. Treat yourself to a glass of ginger water after a day working in the fields, gardening, or playing sports. It's made to replenish your energy.

What You Need

- 1¼ cups (300 mL) cold water
- 1 tablespoon (15 mL) apple cider vinegar
- 2 teaspoons (10 mL) ground ginger
- 1–2 tablespoons (15–30 mL) molasses

What to Do

1. Place the water, vinegar, ginger, and one tablespoon (15 mL) of molasses in a tall glass, jug, or reusable water bottle.
2. Stir or shake to mix well.
3. Add more molasses if it needs to be sweetened.
4. Drink after working up a sweat on a hot day.

Cambric Tea

Grace enjoyed cambric tea during the October blizzard and again on Christmas day. Children, especially, enjoyed the warm drink when older people around them would drink coffee or tea.

Pioneers serving cambric tea wouldn't need to measure. Instead they would just mix boiling water, milk, sugar, and a splash of tea. You can try that or follow this recipe.

Adult supervision required.

What You Need

- 2 tablespoons (30 mL) warm, brewed tea
- 1 teaspoon (5 mL) granulated sugar
- ½ cup (120 mL) boiling water
- ½ cup (120 mL) milk

What to Do

Place the warm tea in a mug or teacup. Stir in the sugar and water. Then add milk and serve.

Buckwheat Pancakes

Even Royal agreed that Almanzo's buckwheat pancakes were the best around—even better than their mother could make.

Buckwheat pancakes taste different than standard wheat flour pancakes, but they are tasty. Buckwheat is not wheat at all, so if you want to make a gluten-free recipe, substitute buckwheat flour for all-purpose flour.

Adult supervision required

What You Need

- ¾ cup (180 mL) buckwheat flour
- ¾ cup (180 mL) all-purpose flour
- 2 teaspoons (10 mL) granulated sugar
- ½ teaspoon (2.5 mL) salt
- 1 teaspoon (5 mL) baking soda
- 1 cup (240 mL) buttermilk*
- 1 egg
- 3 tablespoons (45 mL) butter, melted

* If you don't have buttermilk on hand, make a substitute by placing one tablespoon (15 mL) vinegar or lemon juice in a liquid measuring cup. Then add enough milk to make 1 cup (240 mL). Let sit for five minutes before adding to the recipe.

What to Do

1. In a medium-sized bowl, mix together both flours, sugar, salt, and baking soda.

2. In another bowl, stir together the buttermilk, egg, and melted butter. Then add this mixture to the flour mixture. Stir until well combined.
3. Let the pancake batter sit for 10 minutes.
4. Have an adult preheat griddle (or frying pan) over medium heat, about 350°F (180°C). Use butter or shortening to grease the griddle so the pancakes don't stick.
5. Drop batter on the hot griddle about ¼ cup (60 mL) at a time. Turn the pancake over when bubbles form and the edges begin to cook and appear dry. Cook until the bottoms are golden brown.
6. Serve warm with butter and molasses. You can also try butter with brown sugar or maple syrup.

Clothesline Path

During the blizzards, Pa relied on the rope clothesline to find the house and stable. Pa couldn't see because of the intense wind and snow. It's extremely difficult to judge distance and even location during a blizzard.

Use a rope (or string, or yarn) to create a path to follow blindfolded. Make the path as long as the clothesline and low enough for all participants to hold easily. You might tie it to a porch and a tree or even between two chairs. Once the clothesline is set up, blindfold players and have them use the clothesline for a guide to get to the goal of the other end of the path. For more fun, have participants call out when they think they are halfway and nearly to the goal. See who is closest to being right.

Braided Rag Trivet

Mary braided long scraps of worn-out fabric together. Once the braid was long enough, Laura sewed the braid flat to make a rug. Rugs made the cold, wooden floors cozier for bare feet.

Use these directions to make a braided trivet from old T-shirt scraps. A trivet is a pad to protect your table from hot pots or pans. (You can also use old pillowcases or other scrap fabric. It's OK to mix stretchy material with woven fabric.)
Adult supervision required.

What You Need

- T-shirts or other scrap fabric
- scissors (fabric or sharp scissors work best)
- thread
- needle
- yarn needle
- binder clip or chip/snack clip
- masking or painter's tape (optional)

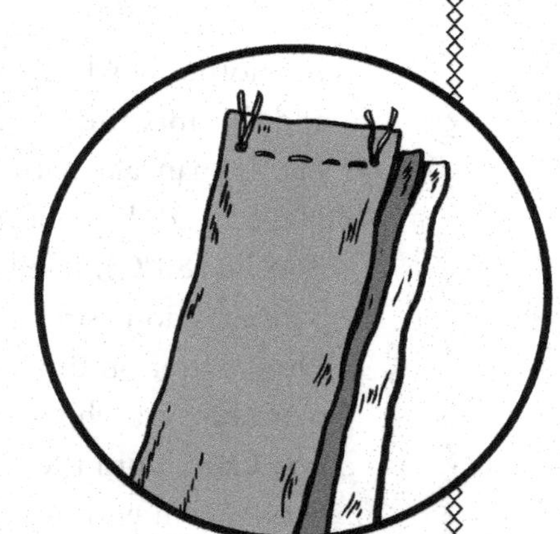

What to Do

1. Cut long fabric strips about 1 inch (2.5 cm) wide.
   - If using a T-shirt, lay it flat on a hard surface, like a table.
   - Trim the hem off the bottom of the shirt in a straight line. Discard.
   - Cut 1-inch (2.5-cm) strips from the bottom of the T-shirt. You can cut through both layers at once if you're careful.
2. Optional: Roll the fabric strips into balls like you would a ball of yarn.
3. Choose three fabric strips. Sew the ends together with needle and thread.
4. Hold the sewed end between your knees or tape it to a table or chair. Braid the fabric strips together. Use a clip to keep the braid together where you have already worked.
5. When you run out of a fabric strip, choose a new color or keep the same color. Overlap the old fabric with about 1 inch (2.5 cm) of the new fabric strip and keep braiding.
6. Continue braiding and attaching new fabric strips as needed.
7. Finish the braid with a knot when it is 8–10 feet long. Then trim the fabric strips to the same length.
8. Thread the yarn needle with a long piece of thread. Bring the ends of the thread together and knot them.
9. Take one end of the braid and fold it to begin to coil the rug in an oval shape. Place the rug face-down. Use the yarn needle to begin lacing thread through the loops of the braid on the face-up "underside" of the rug. Begin

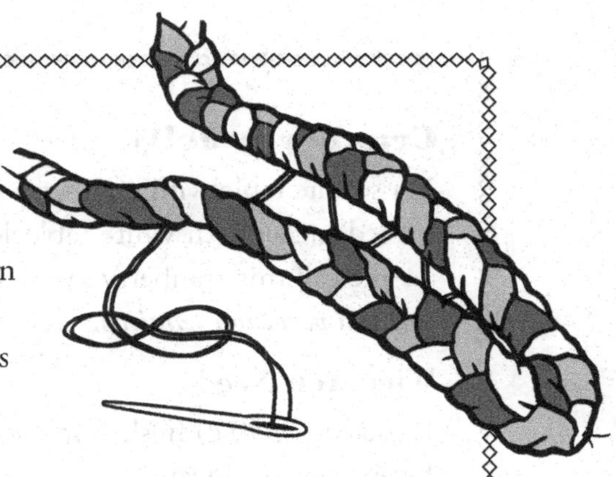

in the first turn so you can attach more of the rug as you go. **Note:** This is not sewing. Don't puncture the fabric with the yarn needle. Instead, push the needle between the fabric strips of the braid.

10. Use the needle and thread to attach two parts of the braid together as pictured below.

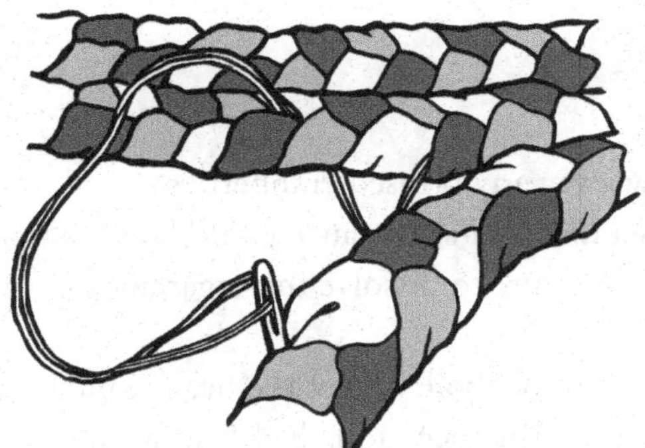

11. As you loop around, you will need to skip an occasional braided strip so the rug will lay flat. It is very important to keep the rug flat as you go.
12. Continue lacing until you have laced the whole braid together. When you lace your final piece to the rug, do it twice to keep it secure. Then tie a knot. Take the knotted thread through a loop one more time, and then snip the thread close to the trivet.
13. Use the trivet under hot pots and pans.

Cranberry Jelly

Ma set the table with cranberry jelly in the center of the table. The red jelly contrasted nicely with white tablecloth for the Christmas feast in May. Today some people call this cranberry sauce. It's a traditional side dish to serve with turkey. *Adult supervision required.*

What You Need

12 ounces (340 g) fresh cranberries
1 cup (240 mL) water
1 cup (240 mL) granulated sugar

What to Do

1. Rinse the cranberries. Throw away any bruised cranberries.
2. Place the water and sugar in a medium-sized sauce pan. Have an adult cook it over medium heat. Stir the mixture to dissolve the sugar and bring it to a boil.
3. Stir in the cranberries and return to a boil. Lower the heat to medium-low. Simmer for about 10 minutes, stirring occasionally. Most of the cranberries should pop.
4. Remove the pan from heat and allow the jelly to cool and thicken a bit. Pour the cranberry jelly into a bowl and refrigerate.
5. Serve cold.

HOUSE TALK

- Ma didn't like Laura helping Pa with field work. What do you think of Ma's thoughts on women working in fields? Why did she think like that?
- The muskrat house gave Pa a clue about the coming winter. How did Pa know so much about nature?
- Laura and Carrie got lost in the tall slough grasses. Then, both girls took responsibility for getting lost (though they didn't tell their parents). What did this show about their personalities?

- Laura knew she would have to sacrifice to help Mary attend college. At first, Laura didn't want to. What changed her mind?
- Why didn't Almanzo plan to go after Lady when she ran away? Why did he go after her?
- Pa bought 4 pounds (1.8 kg) of beef from Mr. Foster. That's the size of a roast you might buy in a grocery store. How long would it last your family?
- Ma was usually cheerful and optimistic, even during hard times, but when she learned the train wasn't coming, she was upset. Why did she let her emotions show this time?
- Almanzo didn't want to sell his seed wheat to Pa. Then he tried to *give* Pa a pail of it. Why did he change his mind? What does this show about Almanzo's character?
- Almanzo Wilder and Cap Garland knew there might not be any wheat when they risked their lives to look for it. Why did they still go?
- Why didn't Almanzo want Mr. Loftus to pay him for such a difficult job?
- Why did Laura awaken the family when she heard the Chinook wind blowing?
- Even once De Smet had food and fuel, what could be some possible lasting effects from the long winter?

Caroline Ingalls. *South Dakota State Historical Society*

Charles Ingalls. *South Dakota State Historical Society*

7

Little Town on the Prairie

DE SMET, DAKOTA TERRITORY

Spring brought new hope for the town and local homesteaders like the Ingalls family after the long, hard winter.

De Smet grew with new buildings and stores. Pa worked in town as a carpenter. A surprising opportunity gave Laura the chance to earn money for Mary's college fund. Laura liked earning money, even if it meant long hours indoors. Soon enough, the family sent Mary to the Iowa College for the Blind.

Laura worked hard in school. A classmate from Laura's past arrived in De Smet. She made trouble for Laura and Carrie at school. She even caused problems with the teacher. But Laura learned living in town had its advantages.

BUILDING DE SMET

De Smet, Dakota Territory, was organized in 1880 as a railroad town. That means it was planned as a stop along the railroad. Its main street, Calumet Avenue, was perpendicular to the railroad tracks of the Chicago and North Western Railway.

The Ingalls family were the first citizens of De Smet. They watched the town grow. Empty building lots in town sold for $50 to $100 when the town was new. Charles Ingalls built on his lot in town (in addition to his homestead) and helped others do the same as a hired carpenter.

Calumet Avenue in De Smet, South Dakota, in its early days. *South Dakota State Historical Society, South Dakota Archives*

DIG DEEPER

Chapter 2

- Calves on farms today learn to drink from a pail the same way Laura taught her calf to drink. It's still a wet and messy job.
- Mary quoted from the Bible when she said, "The Lord is my shepherd." You can read this prayer of comfort in Psalm 23 of the Bible.

Chapter 5

- Laura learned to sew at home and was good enough to get paid for her work. She became a seamstress at the age of 14. Her job was to baste fabric together for shirts. That means she sewed the fabric pieces together in long, temporary stiches. Later, Mrs. White sewed the pieces again using the machine. Then she removed Laura's stitches. Laura also cut and sewed buttonholes. She needed skill and patience to do them well.

Chapter 7

- Mrs. Boast's 14 chickens were quite the gift. The young hens, called pullets, would eventually lay eggs, and the cockerels made a good dinner.

Chapter 8

- The British controlled Fort Ticonderoga in New York State during the Revolutionary War. A group of 83 men, called the Green Mountain Boys, crossed Lake Champlain at dawn while the British soldiers slept. The British surrendered the fort without a shot being fired.
- The community shared the tin dipper for lemonade. People regularly shared from a ladle or dipper then. People didn't have disposable drinking cups. They also didn't understand germs as well as we do today.
- Laura heard a man say Almanzo Wilder's horses were the best in the country (meaning the region—not the whole United States). In *Farmer Boy*, Almanzo thought his father's horses were the best.

Chapter 9

- Ma wanted her family to be dressed in the latest styles. She made sure Mary had all the right dresses for college. Ma even planned the new dress so Mary could wear it with or without a hoopskirt underneath (learn more about hoopskirts on page 19). One of Mary's petticoats used 6 yards (5.4 m) of lace along the bottom. That's 18 feet of lace! Ladies wore several petticoats at once to make their skirts and dresses full.
- The magazine, *Godey's Lady's Book*, was an important resource for women's issues in the 1800s. Its articles focused on home and health, but women also read the magazine for the newest fashions and trends.
- Pa planted the corn and oats as cash crops. He planned to sell them after the harvest. Like many other farmers, Pa wanted to earn money from farming instead of growing just enough for his family.

MARY'S COLLEGE

Mary Ingalls became a student at the Iowa School for the Blind in November 1881. She was 16 years old.

Mary learned a wide variety of academics such as history, geography, philosophy, and botany. Music and industrial courses were also part of her college education. She completed her seven years of study and graduated in 1889. (She likely took one year off due to illness.)

Mary Ingalls graduated from the Iowa School for the Blind of Vinton, Iowa, in 1889. *Historic American Building Society, Library of Congress*

Chapter 10

- Ma was right about Mary's trunk lasting a lifetime. You can still find trunks like hers in antique shops today—nearly 150 years later.
- A trip from De Smet, South Dakota, to Vinton, Iowa, covers more than 400 miles (640 km).

Chapter 12

- Laura remembered the line from Alfred, Lord Tennyson's poem, "The Lotos-Eaters." This showed her knack for words long before she became a published writer. Alfred, Lord Tennyson was a poet during the 19th century. He also wrote the popular poem "The Charge of the Light Brigade."

Chapter 15

- Laura's bitter attitude toward her teacher led to trouble Laura had never imagined. Schoolmates sang Ida and Laura's creative poem. But the poem embarrassed Laura. She never expected others to read it—or sing it! Even when we think our words are private, we never know who will hear or see them.

Laura and Carrie attended the first school of De Smet, South Dakota, as seen here. *Photo © Laura Ingalls Wilder Memorial Society, De Smet, South Dakota*

Chapter 16

- Almanzo Wilder lived in Burke, New York, (near Malone) as a boy. You may have read about his childhood in *Farmer Boy*. His parents sold their valuable farm and moved the family to Spring Valley, Minnesota, in 1875.

Chapter 17

- The John Brown in Laura's history book was an abolitionist trying to stop slavery. Most abolitionists were peaceful. But John Brown used violence. His most famous raid was in Harpers Ferry, Virginia (now West Virginia), in 1859.

John Brown.
Library of Congress

Chapter 19

- Pa acted out his own charade, but no one could guess it. He carried a couple of potatoes and an ax. He wanted people to think of the Commentators on the Acts, which were notes and comments about the Book of Acts from the Bible. Potatoes are sometimes called "taters." Say "common taters on the ax" aloud. It was a play on words.
- Lizzie Bates wrote *Stories from the Moorland*. It was published in 1869.
- Though blind, Mary sent letters home. She learned to write on paper using a grooved slate designed to help blind people write.

Chapter 20

- Laura's favorite poem by Alfred, Lord Tennyson is titled "Maud." Find it online to read the entire poem.
- Quaker meetings are like a church service where people worship God in silence. When (or if) someone attending feels inspired by God to share something, they interrupt the silence by speaking. Historically, the name of the Quaker church was the Society of Friends. Quakers (also called Friends) still meet throughout the United States with many in the mid-Atlantic states, especially Pennsylvania and New Jersey. Others worship around the world, including Europe, Africa, and South America.

Chapter 21

- In the spirit of famous minstrel shows across the United States, five men entertained the town for the final literary event. Historically, minstrels were traveling musicians. In Laura's day, some painted their faces black with exaggerated lips and eyes. They told jokes and sang songs. Just like the De Smet men, minstrel actors (both black and white) made fun of black stereotypes to make people laugh. Minstrel shows and songs were popular at the time, but that doesn't make them right. The shows reinforced racist ideas. It's never OK to laugh at or mock another person because they look, think, talk, or act differently than you.

Chapter 22

- The men who died in the blizzard would likely have lived if they had crawled into the center of the haystack. Hay acts as an insulator, like a pile of blankets.
- In the 1800s, unmarried women often chose to be teachers. Women had few career choices (and some schools would not hire married women). Others, like Ma, chose to stop teaching when they married.

THE ELECTRIC TELEGRAPH

The telegraph connected people over long distances, like phones and computers do today. Telegraphs used electrical signals to send and receive messages called telegrams.

Instead of written letters, telegraphs used Morse code to make words. A series of electric clicks formed dots and dashes. Dots were short clicks, and dashes were long clicks. They represented letters of the alphabet. Telegraph operators sent and received messages. When they received one, they translated it back into words. Then a messenger delivered it to the intended person as a telegram.

Operators sent the messages over cables or wires hanging from telegraph poles, which looked like telephone or cable lines of today. The poles were often set along railroad tracks. They could even be placed in rivers and oceans. By 1866 the first permanent telegraph system was set up across the Atlantic Ocean. Then people could send telegrams between the United States and Europe.

A telegraph operator prints a telegram.
Walden Fawcett, Library of Congress

Chapter 23

- Mr. Owen knew Willie was faking his confusion to avoid work, so he punished him.
- Revival meetings had a special purpose: they focused on salvation more than a regular church service. Reverend Brown wanted people to be sorry for what they did wrong (called "sin") and ask for forgiveness from God. Christians call this process repentance and believed in Laura's day—as they do now—that, because of the death and resurrection of Jesus Christ, God would offer forgiveness and eternal life after death to everyone who repented.

Chapter 24

- Students commonly memorized history, geography, and other subjects in the 1800s. They even completed complicated math problems without paper.
- Carrie recited the poem "Life Sculptor" by George Washington Doane. The poem was titled "The Sculptor Boy," in the *Independent Fifth Reader*, the Ingallses' book.
- Almanzo told Laura of his plans to make a cutter. A cutter is a small sleigh for two people. They were often used for courting—what we call dating today. Almanzo even asked Laura if she'd be interested in a sleigh ride, which would be like a date.

FACT OR FICTION?

The actual date on Laura Ingalls's teaching certificate was December 10, 1883. She was 16 years old. The dates and ages in the story were changed, but still show the need for teachers.

The Dakota Territory's actual age requirement for teachers in 1883 was 18. The district superintendents often overlooked the requirement because of the teacher shortage. Many teachers were younger than 18.

The Laura Ingalls Wilder Historic Home and Museum displays a photo of Laura Ingalls's third-grade teaching certificate. See page 126 for more on teaching certificates.

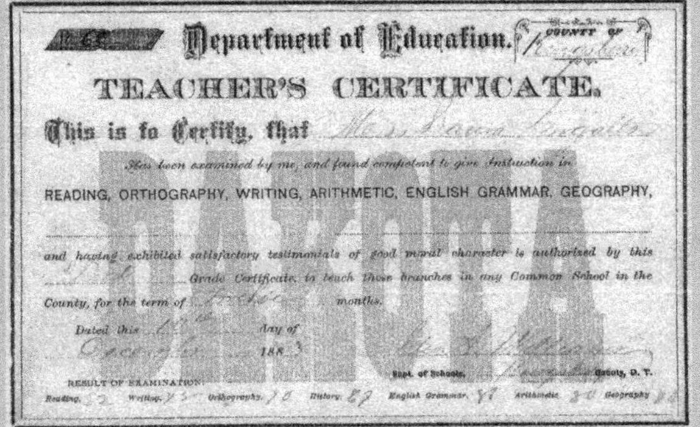

Department of Education. COUNTY OF [illegible]

TEACHER'S CERTIFICATE.

This is to Certify, that [illegible]

Has been examined by me, and found competent to give Instruction in

READING, ORTHOGRAPHY, WRITING, ARITHMETIC, ENGLISH GRAMMAR, GEOGRAPHY,

and having exhibited satisfactory testimonials of good moral character is authorized by this [illegible] Grade Certificate, to teach those branches in any Common School in the County, for the term of [illegible] months.

Dated this [illegible] day of [illegible] 188[illegible]

[illegible] Supt. of Schools, [illegible] County, D. T.

RESULT OF EXAMINATION:

Reading [illegible] Writing [illegible] Orthography [illegible] History [illegible] English Grammar [illegible] Arithmetic [illegible] Geography [illegible]

DAKOTA

Laura Ingalls earned this teaching certificate in 1883. *Photo © Laura Ingalls Wilder Home & Museum, Mansfield, Missouri*

LIVE LIKE LAURA

Declaration!

One man read the Declaration of Independence as part of the Fourth of July celebration. Like many other children then, Laura and Carrie already had it memorized.

Celebrate Independence Day by reading the Declaration of Independence aloud. You can even memorize it like Laura and Carrie.

Chicken Pie with Biscuit Crust

Ma surprised the family with a chicken pie—except she really made it with blackbirds.

Try this hearty pie on a cool day. You can also use pie crust instead of the biscuits to make a chicken pot pie.
Adult supervision required.

What You Need

- 1½ cups (360 mL) of mixed vegetables (mix corn, peas, green beans, carrot coins, or other favorites)
- ½ cup (120 mL) potatoes, peeled and chopped
- ¼ cup (60 mL) butter
- ¼ cup (60 mL) flour
- ½ teaspoon (2.5 mL) salt
- ¼ teaspoon (2.5 mL) pepper
- 1¼ cup (240 mL) chicken broth
- ½ cup (120 mL) milk
- 2 cups (480 mL) cooked chicken, cut into bite-sized pieces
- biscuit dough (canned or homemade from Steps 1–11 on pages 90–91)

What to Do

1. Preheat oven to 425°F (220°C). Butter a pie pan or spray it with cooking spray.
2. Bring water to boil in a medium sauce pan. Place vegetables and potatoes in water and simmer for 8 minutes. Drain.

3. Melt butter in a large saucepan over medium heat. Add flour, salt, and pepper. Stir until well blended.
4. Slowly stir in the chicken broth and milk. Stir frequently. Bring to boil and stir constantly for two minutes, then remove from heat.
5. Place the chicken, vegetables, and potatoes into the pie pan.
6. Pour the mixture into the prepared pie pan. Arrange the dough biscuits in a single layer over the pie with sides almost touching.
7. Bake at 425°F (220°C) for 10 minutes. Cover with aluminum foil so the biscuits don't burn. Then bake for 15 more minutes. Let cool a few minutes before serving.

Name Cards

Laura and her friends chose name card designs at the newspaper office.

Using clip art or your own artistic talent, create your own name cards. It's even more fun to do it in a group and trade name cards with your friends.

What to Do

Create your own name card to reflect your personality and hobbies. You might include an image along with your name. Some people may want to include their contact information. If you want them the size of standard business cards make them 2 inches by 3½-inches (5 cm by 9 cm).

Make each of your name cards unique by decorating them with pencil, marker, paint, stickers, or photos. Or you can use a computer and printer to make them all with the same design. Some computer software even has templates for business cards.

Charades

Everyone laughed at the second literary event's charades.

To play charades, act out a word or phrase without talking and try to get your team to guess it. Props can add to the fun but aren't needed. Themes are also helpful for planning and playing.

Create a Little House theme using words, people, or even book titles from Laura Ingalls Wilder's books—or create your own theme! Write the words on slips of scrap paper if you want to prepare words to be drawn from a bowl or have each person come up with their own words.

Remember, don't talk when giving clues. Instead, act out the word or phrase. These words might help you get started or choose your own:

churn	sewing	tin cup	cabin	sod house
braids	fiddle	sleigh ride	watermelon	wolf
railroad	horse	Jack	school	wagon
hoopskirt	blizzard	beard	malaria	Charlotte

Drop the Handkerchief

At Ben Woodworth's birthday party, the teenagers enjoyed a game of drop the handkerchief. You just need a group of friends and a handkerchief (or bandana or napkin) to play.

Everyone stands in a circle facing inward, except the player with the handkerchief. The person with the handkerchief runs behind the circle and sneakily drops the handkerchief behind another player. He or she can even try to mislead those in the circle by changing how fast and slow he or she runs.

When a player discovers the handkerchief behind them, they must grab it and chase the first player around the circle. The player who dropped the handkerchief (the runner) tries to get around the circle and to the open spot; the chaser tries to tag them before they make it. If the runner makes it safely, the chaser is the next to drop the handkerchief; if the chaser manages to tag the runner in time, the runner has to stay outside the circle and drop the handkerchief again to start the next round.

HOUSE TALK

- Laura and Mary talked about being good. Was Mary truly good if she wanted to be mean but didn't show it?
- Ma never complained about sewing, but Laura figured out Ma didn't like it. How could this help Laura?
- If Mary and her classmates couldn't see her clothes, why did she still need pretty dresses and petticoats?
- Grace cried when Mary went away to college. Why did Laura think Grace shouldn't cry? What do you think?
- Laura had confidence in Miss Wilder's teaching ability since she had a certificate. How does a certificate or degree prepare a person for a job? In what ways doesn't it?
- How was Laura a good friend to Ida Brown before she even knew her?
- Laura told her parents about the name cards but never even hinted she wanted them. Why not?
- How did Mr. Foster surprise the people of De Smet? (You can read about his foolishness in *The Long Winter*.)
- Laura let her grades become less than perfect when she took time away from studying for fun. Was she wrong to take a break from studying?
- Why was Laura excited to go on a sleigh ride date with Almanzo?
- How did Laura feel about being a school teacher? Did Laura have qualities that would make her a good teacher?

Young people enjoyed sleigh rides together. *Marian S. Carson collection, Library of Congress*

8

These Happy Golden Years

DE SMET, DAKOTA TERRITORY

Laura left home to become a school teacher when she was just 15 years old in the story (in real life she was 16, which was still young to leave her home and family). Being away from her family was harder than Laura expected. Laura was smart, but teaching was still hard. Earning money to help Mary pleased Laura. She looked forward to the weekends when she visited her family.

Each Friday Almanzo drove his small sleigh to pick up Laura from school. She appreciated the rides home so she could see her family.

Laura loved the fun and wonder of her teenage years when she wasn't working. Singing school and buggy rides kept her busy with friends. As Laura grew up, she learned just how special her own family was and the importance of having good friends.

PRAIRIE SCHOOL

In the 1880s some people attended colleges called "normal schools" that trained them to be teachers. But not all teachers received this special training.

With so many pioneers moving west to unsettled areas, more and more schools were built. Every school needed a teacher. Regular townspeople like store owners, farmers, and even older students were hired to teach on the frontier. Students learned arithmetic (math), reading (including spelling and grammar), geography, history, and much more.

There usually weren't enough school supplies. Families provided their own textbooks, and siblings often shared books. Some families didn't have enough money for even one schoolbook. Those children usually learned to read from the Bible. Since teachers and students didn't have a lot of spare paper, students memorized a lot of information and used slates and blackboards for lessons.

DIG DEEPER

Chapter 1

- The curtain around Laura's sofa gave her some privacy while sleeping.

Chapter 2

- Laura's height concerned her; she wondered if her students would respect a short teacher. Three of Laura's students were older than her. It's likely those students were taller than her too.
- It was cold outside and not much warmer inside the schoolhouse. With spaces between the wall boards and more gaps between the floorboards, it was no wonder they were so cold!

FACT OR FICTION?

How tall was Half-Pint? As a grown woman, Laura Ingalls Wilder stood just over 5 feet (152 cm) tall. (Some resources state she was even shorter.) Pa called her Half-Pint, even as a teenager, because she was so small—like half of a pint. (A pint equals two cups, or 480 ml.)

Chapter 3

- Mrs. Brewster wanted to return to the East. She may have felt depressed and lonely. Mrs. Brewster didn't enjoy Laura's company or appreciate her help around the house.

Chapter 4

- Laura didn't want Mary Power to think Almanzo was "beauing" Laura home. That would mean he was her beau, or boyfriend. Laura quickly corrected Mary.

Chapter 7

- Laura didn't want to trick Almanzo, so she finally explained to him she only rode with him to get home. She didn't want him to think she wanted him as a beau.
- Mrs. Brewster threatened her husband with a knife. She wanted him to at least think about going back East. Mr. Brewster likely didn't have any way to make a living without the claim, so he couldn't leave.

Chapter 8

- Lady and Prince's breath froze during the cold ride. Ice covered their nostrils and made it hard for them to breathe. Almanzo didn't pull off the pieces of ice because that would hurt the horses. Instead, he held his hand over their noses, and their warm breath melted the ice.
- Almanzo became clumsy and Laura sleepy on the cold ride home. These are both symptoms of the onset of hypothermia. Read about the risks of extreme cold on page 100.

Chapter 10

- Almanzo told Laura about his first horse. You can read about his boyhood adventures with Starlight in *Farmer Boy*.

Chapter 13

- Uncle Tom was Ma's brother. During his visit, he told all the family news. Like many others, Uncle Tom wanted to find gold in the West.
- When Cap began teasing Mary Power, she worried Cap would learn her secret. She wore a clip-on hair piece, called a switch. She used the switch in addition to her own hair and made a knot (fancy bun) with the switch.

FACT OR FICTION?

Laura Ingalls's first school was actually the Bouchie School, not the Brewster School. Some people think Laura Ingalls Wilder changed the name of the school because of scandals related to the Bouchie family.

The Bouchie (Brewster) School. *Photo © Laura Ingalls Wilder Memorial Society, De Smet, South Dakota*

Chapter 14

- Laura stayed with Mrs. McKee and her daughter, Mattie, on their claim. Mrs. McKee invited Laura to stay with her as one of the family. She paid Laura, but Mrs. McKee didn't expect her to be hired help working all day long.

Chapter 16

- Laura's reputation earned her even more work. Next, she worked with Miss Bell in her millinery and dressmaking shop. A milliner makes hats.

Chapter 17

- Cap asked Laura if she wanted to go for a sleigh ride with Almanzo. The colts wouldn't calm down enough to let Almanzo knock on her door.
- Almanzo talked about breaking horses. It may sound cruel, but it just meant they were training the horses. Before a person can ride a horse or use one to pull a wagon or buggy, the horse needs to be trained. It takes a lot of time and patience. Almanzo worked with teams that were fast and hard to control, but he was patient with them.

Chapter 18

- With spring's arrival, Pa wanted to move to the claim. The claim was closer to the Perry School. Pa oversaw building the schoolhouse and others helped too.
- Laura earned $25 each of the three months she taught at the Perry School. Her pay would have been the same whether she had 3 students or 30. It was a good wage as a teacher in Kingsbury County, and it helped her family buy an organ.

Organists use their hands and feet to play organs. Music is made by moving air through the pipes.
John Vachon, Library of Congress

Chapter 19

- Laura's hair hung below her knees. In the 1800s, many women had long hair. Most girls braided it, and young ladies and women typically pulled their hair up.

Chapter 20

- Farmers milk their cows on a schedule—typically every 12 hours. If a cow's udder gets too full of milk, she becomes very uncomfortable. Regular milking also helps the cow make a large amount of milk. Today some farmers milk more than twice a day but always on a schedule.

Chapter 21

- Almanzo named his new horses Skip and Barnum. The popular circus showman Phineas T. Barnum inspired the second horse's name. Almanzo wondered how Laura would like the "circus" he drove.
- Are you surprised that Almanzo and Laura rode 60 miles (100 km) in a day? Skip and Barnum were high-energy horses that loved to run. You might remember when riding with the covered wagon, Pa only drove his team about 20 miles (32 km) in a day. Without a heavy load, horses can travel much faster and farther.

FACT OR FICTION?

Readers recognize Nellie Oleson for the bully she was. Nellie represented three real rivals from Laura Ingalls Wilder's childhood.

Nellie Owens and Genevieve Masters lived in Walnut Grove, Minnesota (also known as Plum Creek). Nellie's father owned a store. Wilder described Nellie and her brother Willie as "rude and selfish." Genevieve liked to brag about her New York connections.

Wilder's third adversary, Stella Gilbert, lived a couple of miles away from Laura's home in De Smet, Dakota Territory. Like the fictional Nellie Oleson, Stella often went on buggy rides with Laura and Almanzo.

Chapter 22

- As more people settled in De Smet, the town needed a larger schoolhouse (see the original building on page 112). Grammar and high school students (equivalent of first through eighth graders) attended classes in the new, two-story schoolhouse in 1885. In 1887, a ninth grade was added as four students prepared for graduation. The new schoolhouse included four classrooms. Each classroom was 29 feet by 29 feet (9 m by 9 m).

Chapter 23

- Both Laura and Ida wore their rings on their first (index) fingers. Today most women wear engagement rings on their ring fingers, not their first fingers.

The Laura Ingalls Wilder Museum in Walnut Grove, Minnesota, sells this replica of Laura's engagement ring. *Courtesy of Laura Ingalls Wilder Museum, Walnut Grove, Minnesota*

Chapter 24

- Almanzo and Royal visited their parents in Spring Valley, Minnesota. You can still see the Wilders' barn and visit the church they attended there.
- The Ingalls family stayed in their own home that winter. During previous winters in Dakota Territory they lived in the surveyors' house and the Ingallses' building in town.
- Read about the Indian Territory and Plum Creek Christmases in *Little House on the Prairie* and *On the Banks of Plum Creek.*

TEACHING CERTIFICATE

Dakota Territory required those who wanted to teach to take an exam. Those who passed earned graded certificates. The grade earned didn't show which grades you could teach. Instead, it told how well you did and how long your certificate would last. However, the school superintendent sometimes changed the length of a certificate or ignored the age requirement for teaching.

The law changed from year to year, but in 1883 those who earned a third-grade certificate could teach for 6 to 12 months (depending on the score). A second-grade certificate meant you scored better on the exam and could teach for 18 months. The best was a first-grade certificate. With that, a teacher could teach for a term of two years.

Chapter 26

- Laura's second-grade teaching certificate let her teach for a year. Though she had earned a certificate before, this was her first teaching exam in a group setting. You can see Laura Ingalls's teaching certificate on page 115.
- Laura knew education was important. She was smart enough to graduate. However, Mr. Owen didn't know Laura would return to school after teaching, so he didn't give her special lessons and exams required for graduation. Laura was disappointed, but she did not complain. You can read more about school requirements on the opposite page.

Chapter 28

- Laura's income really did help the family. Not only did they have an organ for Mary, Pa bought Ma a sewing machine too. They weren't rich, but they were able to buy some things they didn't *need.*
- The beautiful fireworks that light up our skies aren't a new technology. Most historians say fireworks were invented in China more than a thousand years ago. The United States celebrated its first birthday with fireworks, bells, and parades on July 4, 1777; fireworks have been part of America's Independence Day celebrations ever since.

Chapter 29

- Today circling winds with dangerous funnels are called tornadoes. The area of De Smet saw multiple tornadoes during 1884. Records show that "three great water-spouts were seen west of De Smet" on August 28, 1884.

Chapter 31

- When Almanzo asked Laura if she wanted women's rights, he meant the right to vote in an election. Though she said she didn't care about voting, Laura did care about independence and often had forward-thinking ideas.
- As a bride, Laura planned to wear her best dress made of black cashmere. Ma and Laura didn't have time to sew a special wedding dress.

Chapter 33

- Laura Ingalls and Almanzo Wilder married on August 25, 1885. They kept the wedding so small that even Ma and Pa didn't go. Almanzo and Laura didn't want to be unfair to Almanzo's family since they couldn't attend. However, Ma did plan a special wedding dinner for the newlyweds.
- Almanzo could have built Laura a simple claim shanty. Instead, he built a beautiful painted house with a large room, bedroom, and pantry. Almanzo paid careful attention to the pantry. He included many thoughtful details in the room just to make Laura happy.
- Laura stored the butter in the cellar because it would be the coolest place in the house.
- Laura Ingalls Wilder ended the eight-volume Little House series on the evening of Laura and Almanzo's wedding. Together, they had hopes and dreams of their future. Learn more about *The First Four Years* on pages 135–136.

SCHOOL REQUIREMENTS

Children ages 7 to 20 could attend school when Laura was a student. But many children did not go to school. In 1883, only children ages 10 to 14 were *required* to attend school in Dakota Territory. Even then, they only had to go to school for twelve weeks each school year.

Some children, even ages 10 to 14, didn't attend school because they received private instruction from a parent or tutor. Others lived too far away or were physically unable to go.

During her childhood, Laura Ingalls learned in many different ways at various times–from her parents, in a schoolhouse, and on her own–because learning was important to her and her family. But Laura didn't graduate, which was common then. Even without a diploma, she later had a writing career for a newspaper and became a bank loan officer. She's most famous for the award-winning Little House books she wrote, which have been translated into many languages around the world.

LIVE LIKE LAURA

Pack Up!

Laura packed very little, despite expecting she'd be away for two months. She took only a dress, underclothes, and her school books, though she didn't expect to return home.

Pretend you need to leave your family for two months. You can only take one backpack. Carefully decide what you absolutely need and take it with you. Make it all fit into your backpack.

Countdown

Laura worked through just one day at a time during her stay with the Brewsters. She crossed off marks in her notebook when she was done studying.

Create a countdown of your own. First decide what you want to count the days until. It might be a holiday, birthday, summer vacation, or the first day of school.

Use a calendar to count the number of days until the event. Then design your countdown. You can use any shape as a symbol for each day. It could be simple circles, stars, or something related to your special event like a gift for a birthday party, flip-flops for summer camp, or a pencil for school. Draw or use a computer to design your countdown.

Once it's ready, color one symbol each day as a way to look forward to your special event. When all of your symbols are filled in, celebrate!

Writing Challenge

On Laura's first day back in school as a student, she learned of the composition assignment. She used her recess time to write her essay. Not everyone can complete a composition in so little time, but it's fun to try.

Write a short essay. Choose one of the topics below. If you are uncertain about a word, use a dictionary like Laura to learn more about it, but use your own ideas too.

Writing Topics: family, respect, heroism, courage, trust, independence, optimism, compassion

House Count Challenge

Almanzo and Laura spent many Sunday afternoons on buggy rides. After one ride, Almanzo commented that many settlers were coming to the area because they had seen six houses in 40 miles (64 km).

Go for a walk, bike ride, or car ride. How many homes can you count in 1 mile (1.6 km)? If that same number of houses per mile continued for 40 miles (64 km), how many houses would there be?

Three Blind Mice in Rounds

During singing school, Laura, Almanzo, and the other students sang "Three Blind Mice" in rounds. Because the groups began and ended at different times, they created a beautiful and complex sound—and they had a lot of fun while they did it.

Sing "Three Blind Mice" with others in rounds. First divide the friends into three groups. (It's OK if you only have one person in each group.) Each group will sing the song three times in row. Plan which group will go first, second, and third. Only the first group begins. When the first group begins "See how they run" the second group starts signing from the beginning. The third group begins when the first group starts "They all ran after the farmer's wife." Repeat for more fun.

Popcorn Balls

Ma used Laura's fresh popcorn to make popcorn balls as part of their Christmas celebration.

Try this old-fashioned molasses popcorn ball recipe for a treat like Laura made. Be sure to use butter or cooking spray on your hands to keep the molasses mixture from sticking to them. You'll need a candy thermometer or instant thermometer for this recipe.

Adult supervision required.

What You Need

- 8 cups (1,820 mL) freshly popped, plain popcorn (½ cup or 120 mL unpopped kernels)
- ½ cup (120 mL) granulated sugar
- ½ cup (120 mL) molasses
- ⅓ cup (80 mL) water
- 1 tablespoon (15 mL) butter
- 1 tablespoon (15 mL) vinegar
- ¼ teaspoon (1 mL) baking soda

What to Do

1. Grease an extra-large bowl with cooking spray or oil. Place the popped popcorn in the bowl. Set it aside.
2. In a large saucepan, mix together the sugar, molasses, water, butter, and vinegar. Have an adult cook it over medium heat. Do *not* stir the molasses mixture while it cooks.
3. Use a candy thermometer to monitor the temperature of the mixture. When the mixture reaches 235°F (115°C), remove from heat. Stir in the baking soda and mix well.
4. Pour the molasses mixture over the popcorn. Stir the molasses with a large spoon until the popcorn is evenly coated with molasses.
5. Grease your hands with butter or cooking spray.
6. Once the mixture has cooled enough to handle, use your hands to form 3-inch (8-cm) balls. Place them on waxed paper.
7. To store, wrap popcorn balls in plastic wrap or baggies.

Beaded Bracelet

Mary sent home a gift of a bracelet made of beads. You can make your own beaded bracelet. It can be as simple as a single strand or a bracelet made with two strands with these directions. Try to make the pattern designed by Mary or design your own for fun.

What You Need

- elastic jewelry thread or strong thread
- small beads
- scissors

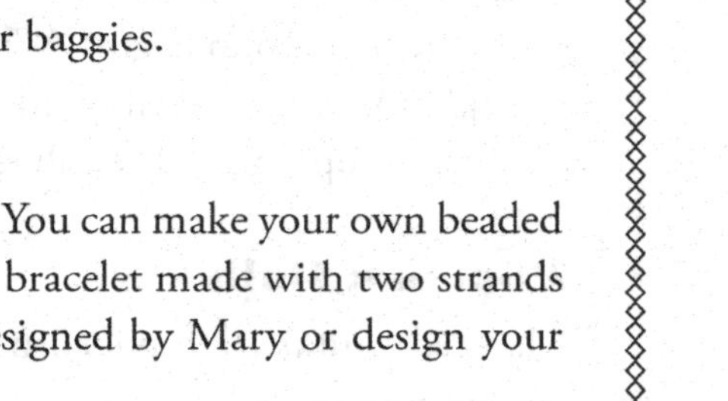

What to Do

1. Cut two 10-inch (25-cm) lengths (or longer) of jewelry thread. Tie one end of each thread together in a knot.
2. Begin a pattern of five beads on one strand of thread. Repeat the pattern on the second strand of thread.
3. Thread both strands through a single bead.

4. Repeat the pattern until the bracelet is the length you want it, then tie the ends in a knot. Finish the bracelet by tying the two tied ends together. Trim any extra thread.

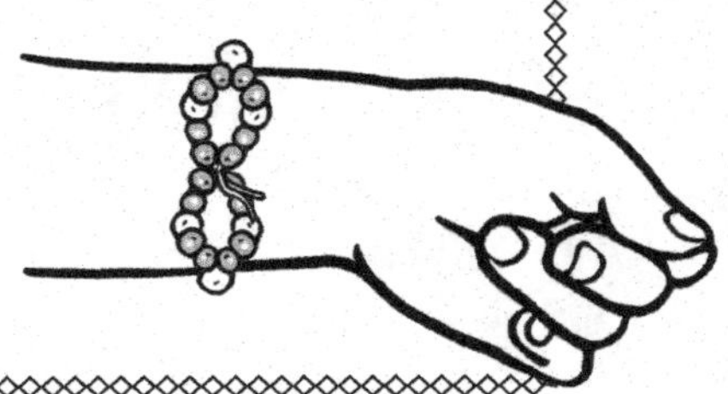

HOUSE TALK

- Mrs. Brewster didn't want to live on the prairie. How did her attitude make her situation worse?
- Laura never complained about living with the Brewsters. How did Almanzo and her parents know it was a bad situation?
- Mrs. Brewster threatened her husband and disliked Laura. Should Laura have stayed? Why do you think she stayed when the situation didn't get any better?
- Why would Almanzo risk the long ride in such cold weather to pick up Laura when he knew she wasn't interested in him being her beau?
- Laura allowed her students to study at the stove. Why didn't they fool around, even though they were out of their seats and regular routine?
- Would Laura have gone sleighing with Almanzo if he had come sooner?
- Mrs. McKee didn't want to live on the claim alone with her daughter. When Laura returned home early, why do you think Mrs. McKee didn't get someone else to stay with her?
- How did college help Mary?
- Think about Mrs. Brewster and Mrs. McKee. They were both lonely on their claims. Why did they respond so differently?
- Riding behind Almanzo's horses thrilled Laura. Can you name other times Laura showed her adventurous spirit in the Little House books?
- During the first Christmas in the new church, Laura received an ivory-backed hairbrush and comb. If the gift came from Almanzo, why didn't he tell her?
- The family enjoyed going to church for Christmas. How would you feel if you couldn't celebrate Christmas, or another special holiday, in your traditional way?
- How do you know Almanzo and Laura were not disappointed they couldn't have a big wedding?

PART 2

LIFE BEYOND LITTLE HOUSE

"I hate to write the end of the story. No, not the end! No story is ever ended!"

—Laura Ingalls Wilder, *Missouri Ruralist*, 1917

Laura and Almanzo Wilder married on August 25, 1885. This picture was taken the next winter. *Photo © Laura Ingalls Wilder Memorial Society, De Smet, South Dakota*

The First Four Years

DE SMET, DAKOTA TERRITORY

Almanzo had both a homestead and a tree claim. He built a cozy house on the tree claim, and then he and Laura finally began their life together.

Laura had always helped Ma with housework. Now Laura did it by herself. Manly worked hard on the farm. Sometimes Laura helped with Almanzo's fieldwork just as she had helped Pa as a girl.

Almanzo and Laura persevered through their first years together. Despite the disasters, they still had a blessing—a baby named Rose.

A DIFFERENT KIND OF LITTLE HOUSE

As you read *The First Four Years*, you might notice some confusing differences from the other Little House books. It might help you to understand more about this book.

First, Laura Ingalls Wilder ended the Little House series after Laura and Almanzo married in *These Happy Golden Years*. She didn't write *The First Four Years* as part of the Little House series. It was published as an ending to the Little House books, but Wilder didn't plan it that way.

Second, Laura Ingalls Wilder wrote this book for adult readers. The first eight books in the Little House series have a similar tone. This book is written for a different audience, so it *is* different. Though the characters are familiar to Little House readers, it's a grown-up story.

Third, Wilder only wrote a first draft of this book. She never revised the manuscript. She never tried to have it published, though she could have.

Writers sometimes call a book's first draft a "sloppy copy." It takes many revisions for a first draft to become a final draft that they are proud of. That's how we see great writing.

Wilder's daughter, Rose Wilder Lane, was a professional writer and worked closely with her mother to edit the first eight Little House books. But she never edited this book. It was edited prior to publication but not by Laura or Rose.

And finally, the book was published posthumously. That means it was published after Laura Ingalls Wilder's death. Laura's daughter, Rose, gave the unrevised manuscript to a man named Roger Lea MacBride after Laura's death. He was like a grandson to Rose, but not an actual relative. It was only after Rose's death that he told an editor at Harper & Row (now HarperCollins) about the manuscript. *The First Four Years* was published in 1971—28 years after *These Happy Golden Years* was published.

DIG DEEPER

Chapter 1

- Manly was Laura's nickname for Almanzo. When they were courting, Almanzo explained that his parents called him Manzo and his brother called him Mannie. Laura misunderstood the nickname and called him Manly. In real life, Laura had a nickname, too. Manly used his wife's middle name, Elizabeth, to come up with the nickname of Bessie. Even their daughter Rose called Laura "Mama Bess."
- Manly and Laura went for a drive and talked. They were already engaged to be married when Laura surprised Manly. She told him that she didn't want to marry a farmer—the job Manly had

A DIFFERENT LAURA?

Laura seems different at the beginning of *The First Four Years* than she did during *These Happy Golden Years*. With Laura's changes, the tone–or feeling–of the story changes too.

Laura is optimistic in *These Happy Golden Years*. She trusts Almanzo, especially as a farmer and horseman. In the other Little House books, Laura was happy to help Pa with farm work. She didn't have to. Ma might have preferred that Laura not work in the fields, yet Laura helped care for the animals and worked in the fields during harvest.

The character named Laura in *The First Four Years* said she didn't want to marry a farmer. She was concerned about the hard work of farming and lack of financial stability.

Remember, *The First Four Years* wasn't written as part of the Little House series. It was a new story. Like the other books, it was somewhat fictionalized. We don't know if Laura Ingalls Wilder changed the main character's view and tone for something her adult readers would like or if it reflected her personal experience and feelings.

had all his life and the one he always wanted. Manly compromised and asked her to try farming for three years.

- Laura Ingalls and Almanzo Wilder really did marry on August 25, 1885. Reverend Edward Brown officiated the ceremony in his home. Ida Brown, along with her fiancé, Elmer McConnell, attended the wedding.
- In her new home, Laura saw the churn and dasher, used for making butter. Laura looked forward to more cream from Manly's cow when she was "fresh." A fresh cow has recently had a new calf. She gives the most milk and cream during this time.
- Manly built the house on the tree claim. He also planted the young trees Laura admired. On a tree claim, instead of farming the land as you would on a homestead, you had to plant trees and keep them alive.
- Manly bought two new horses to give Skip and Barnum a break. Have you heard the phrase, "Many hands make light work"? It's the same with horses. Several horses working together go faster than just one horse, and each horse does less work.
- Manly made walls of hay by stacking the hay close together. It insulated the barn for winter. He even cut holes in the hay and placed windows over them to keep out cold air and let in light.
- Laura and Manly celebrated their birthdays just one week apart in February. Laura Ingalls was born February 7, 1867, in Pepin, Wisconsin. Almanzo Wilder was born February 13, 1859 (or 1857), near Malone, New York. See more information about Almanzo's birth date in the sidebar.

WHEN WAS ALMANZO WILDER BORN?

Books about Almanzo Wilder report his birthday as February 13, 1857. Even his headstone in Mansfield, Missouri, lists that date. But some researchers wonder if this is accurate. Multiple census records show he was likely born in 1859.

A census reports basic information about the population. In 1860, the census recorded Almanzo as a 1-year-old. Then the 1870 census stated Almanzo's age as 11, and in 1875 the census said he was 16. If these are accurate, he would have been born in 1859. Census records often contained errors, but it would be highly unlikely for three reports in a row to be wrong *and* consistent.

A likely reason for the birth-year confusion is homesteaders had to be 21 to file a claim. No proof was needed. *The Long Winter* explains how Almanzo's age was a secret since he was only 19 when he filed for his claim instead of 21. It's possible Almanzo just continued to say his "older" age so his homestead claim wouldn't be taken away.

We don't need to know Almanzo Wilder's actual birth year, but it's interesting to think about.

- Laura was quite sick and even fainted when she stood up. She was pregnant! Laura was sicker than most women during pregnancy.
- Trees needed water to grow, but the weather was too dry. Manly added manure around the base of the trees as fertilizer. It wasn't water, but animal waste adds nutrients to the soil. Farmers still use manure as fertilizer today.
- Manly bought his farming equipment with loans. The mowing machine, hay rake, and binder put Manly into debt. He also purchased Skip and Barnum using loans.

BORROWED MONEY

Farmers often purchased farming equipment with loans when they didn't have the cash. The loans were sometimes called notes or mortgages. Bank loans aren't free though. Extra money called interest must be paid back in addition to the borrowed money. A chattel mortgage is a special mortgage used for property that moves, such as livestock (unlike a barn, house, or even land).

A mower cut hay faster than cutting it by hand. *Louis Maurer, Library of Congress*

- A 20-minute hail storm destroyed the Wilders' wheat crop. They lost the $3,000 harvest. Hail "planted" the seed (the part people eat and the seed of the crop) into the ground. But it couldn't grow in Dakota Territory in the fall.
- Today $3,000 would be worth almost $80,000. Now, farmers often need more than a year to earn that much money. Like Manly, they must pay for expensive equipment too.

- The bills were due. Manly took out another loan called a mortgage to pay the bills. Manly also found a renter for the tree claim. They would have to leave the cozy house and move to the homestead.

Chapter 2

- Guns often "kick" back when the trigger is pulled. A hunter puts the back side of a rifle, called the stock, to his or her shoulder. This stops it from moving too much. When Manly forgot to do this, he got a bloody nose *and* missed the goose.
- During the 1800s, most women gave birth at home. Laura did too, but she didn't do it alone. Manly brought Laura's mother for help. Then Ma sent Manly to get Mrs. Power from town too. Soon enough the doctor came to help.
- Doctors often gave women chloroform during childbirth. The treatment gave Laura double vision and caused her to sleep through the birth of her daughter.
- Mr. Boast's offer to adopt baby Rose scared Laura even though they were good friends.

Chapter 3

- Laura thought she had a cold. She soon realized she was wrong. She nearly died from diphtheria. Manly was not as sick as Laura. But he didn't take the time he needed to get better. Manly's weak health eventually led to a stroke and limited his strength and use of his legs. Almanzo Wilder walked with a limp all his life.
- Since Manly couldn't work both the tree claim and the homestead, he and Laura sold the homestead and moved back to the tree claim.
- Laura usually left money decisions up to Manly. When Laura sold her colt, however, she chose how to spend the money. She bought sheep with Cousin Peter.

Chapter 4

- It'd been three years since they married, so Laura and Manly talked about the farm. They agreed to try one more year of farming because one good crop would make them a success.
- Mr. Sheldon lent his set of Waverley books to Laura (spelled "Waverly" in *The First Four Years*). These books by Sir Walter Scott told some of the history of Scotland, including the famous story *Ivanhoe.*

A field of wheat is almost ready for harvest. *Author's collection*

- It took Peter and Manly over an hour to move the sheep just 400 yards (370 m), which would take most people about five minutes to walk. The winds literally blew the sheep over!
- The coupons from the grocery store were different than coupons today. The coupon books were like a loan from the store. Just like a bank loan, these loans had to be repaid with interest (an extra fee). The coupon loans were the grocery store's way to make sure people still shopped, even if they didn't have cash. It helped the store *and* the customers. Most homesteaders struggled to farm and were deep in debt.
- Manly had to show the government he had proved up (improved) his tree claim; he couldn't do that since the trees died. Other people would have the chance to buy or live on his land. Since Manly wanted to keep the land, he filed a pre-emption (preemption). The pre-emption gave Manly six months to claim and buy the land so he could continue to live on it without having improved it yet.
- Shortly after the death of their son, another tragedy struck the Wilders: Laura and Manly's house burned down. Laura quickly realized the fire was out of control. She took Rose and their deed box (which held important papers) to safety. Mr. Sheldon rescued dishes, silver, and the bread plate from the fire.
- The family moved into the new house in September. Laura and Manly were hopeful of their future together.

DIPHTHERIA TODAY

Diphtheria is a highly contagious infection and spreads mostly through coughing and sneezing. The bacteria destroys healthy tissue in the respiratory system and makes it hard to breathe. Sometimes it leads to damage to other organs like the heart and kidneys. It can even lead to paralysis.

Doctors use medication to treat diphtheria today. Even with treatment, though, some people who contract diphtheria die. Thanks to a vaccine developed in the early 1900s, however, sickness and death from diphtheria are significantly less. It is now rare in the United States and other developed countries.

THE BABY BOY

Laura and Almanzo Wilder's son was born on July 11, 1889, according to De Smet newspapers. He weighed 10 pounds (4.5 kg). A month later, the same newspaper reported his death on August 7. He did not have a name. The family buried the baby in the De Smet cemetery in an unmarked grave. A marker in the cemetery now reads "Infant Wilder."

LIVE LIKE LAURA

Grow a Geranium

Laura wanted to make her new house pretty. She planned to plant geranium flowers in cans to decorate the window sills. You can plant your own flowers too.

What You Need

- pebbles
- large, clean tin can
- garden soil
- geranium (or other houseplant)
- ribbon (optional)
- water

What to Do

1. Place a 1–2-inch (2.5–5-cm) layer of pebbles in the bottom of the can. Add soil but leave room for the plant's roots.
2. Add a geranium to the soil and fill in additional soil as needed.
3. Tie a ribbon around the can to make it festive.
4. Water the geranium and set it in a sunny window or outside.
5. Check the soil daily for moisture. Water the plant when the soil is dry (possibly every day).

Corn Bread

Laura had to cook her first meal as a married woman for the threshers. She served pork, potatoes, and navy beans. To make sure there was plenty of food, she made corn bread to go with the loaf of bread from her Ma.
Adult supervision required.

What You Need

- 1 cup (240 mL) all-purpose flour
- 1 cup (240 mL) corn meal
- ¼ cup (60 mL) granulated sugar
- 1 tablespoon (15 mL) baking powder
- 1 teaspoon (1 mL) salt
- 1 cup (240 mL) milk
- ¼ cup (60 mL) vegetable oil
- 1 egg, beaten

What to Do

1. Preheat oven to 425°F (220°C).

2. Use cooking spray or butter to grease a 9" by 9" baking pan.
3. Mix the flour, corn meal, sugar, baking powder, and salt together in a large bowl.
4. In a medium-sized bowl, stir the milk, oil, and egg together. Pour the wet ingredients into the large bowl with the dry ingredients. Mix with a large spoon until just mixed.
5. Spread the mixture into the prepared pan. Bake for 20–25 minutes in the preheated oven.
6. Serve warm.

Pieplant Pie

Laura made pieplant pie, also known as rhubarb pie, for dessert. The sour taste was quite a shock. Try this recipe—but don't forget the sugar!
Adult supervision required.

What You Need

- 1¼ cup (300 mL) granulated sugar
- ⅓ cup (80 mL) all-purpose flour
- ½ teaspoon (2.5 mL) cinnamon
- 6 cups (1440 mL) chopped rhubarb stalks*
- prepared pie crust (top and bottom)

* Caution: Note that rhubarb leaves are poisonous. Most grocery stores will remove the leaves from the stalks, but make sure you don't accidentally include any in your chopped rhubarb stalks.

What to Do

1. Preheat oven to 375°F (190°C).
2. Mix together the sugar, flour, and cinnamon in a large bowl. Gently stir in the chopped rhubarb. Set it aside.
3. Line a 9-inch (23-cm) pie plate with a bottom pie crust. Pour the pie filling in the shell. Add the top crust or a lattice crust and crimp the edge together with the edge of the bottom crust (a lattice crust lets the pretty pink filling show). If using a full crust, cut slits in the top pie crust for ventilation.
4. Cover the edges of the pie with foil to keep them from burning.

5. Bake the pie for 25 minutes in a preheated oven. Then remove foil. Bake for an additional 20–30 minutes until the filling bubbles and the top is golden brown.
6. Remove from the oven and cool on a wire rack.

Homemade Bread

Bread was important for all pioneers, including the Ingalls and Wilder families. Laura would have mastered bread making at her ma's side. For Manly and Laura's shared birthday celebration, Laura kept the meal simple. She served meat, vegetables, and bread, with birthday cake for dessert.

Baking your own bread takes time, but it's delicious! You can use a stand mixer with a dough hook to mix and knead the bread dough. Or you can use a mixing bowl and knead the dough on a counter.

Adult supervision required.

What You Need

- 3 tablespoons (45 mL) granulated sugar
- 1 cup (240 mL) warm water (not hot water)
- 2¼ teaspoon (11 mL) active dry yeast or 1½ teaspoons (6 mL) instant yeast
- ¾ teaspoon (3.5 mL) salt
- 2 tablespoons (30 mL) oil (vegetable or canola oil work well)
- 3–3½ cups (720–840 mL) flour (bread flour or all-purpose flour)

What to Do

1. Place the sugar and water in a large bowl or the bowl of a stand mixer. Stir in the yeast. If using active dry yeast, allow a few minutes for the yeast to proof (become foamy). You may continue adding ingredients immediately if using instant yeast.
2. Stir the salt and oil into the bowl.
3. Carefully measure flour. Fill a measuring cup by sprinkling the flour into the cup. Then scrape the flour level by scraping the flat edge of a knife along the edge of the cup. Do not scoop the flour (see more about measuring flour on page 35).
4. Stir in 3 cups (720 mL) of flour, mixing after each cup. When you've added 3 cups (720 mL) of flour, stop and knead it for three minutes (either by

hand or using a stand mixer with a dough hook). If the bread dough is still sticky, sprinkle in more flour, one tablespoon (15 mL) at a time. Allow the dough to mix well after each addition. (If using a stand mixer, you want the dough to stick to the bottom of the bowl but not the sides.)

5. Knead the dough for 5 to 7 minutes total with the stand mixer or seven minutes total by hand.
6. Place the bread dough in a lightly oiled bowl. Then, turn the dough upside down so all of the dough is coated with oil. Cover the bowl with a damp cloth. Allow the dough to rise for one hour. It should nearly double in size.
7. Gently punch the dough to deflate it. This releases air bubbles.
8. Lightly sprinkle a counter or table with flour. Knead the dough a few times and then shape it into a loaf.
9. Place dough into a well oiled loaf pan. Allow the dough to rise for about 30 minutes. The dough should rise to the pan's rim or just a bit above.
10. Bake at 350°F (180°C) in a preheated oven for 30 minutes. Remove the bread from the pan and place on a cooling rack.
11. To make a softer crust, butter the dome of the bread. Allow to cool before slicing.

Frozen Milk

The blizzard struck while Manly worked in the barn. When he finally made it to the house, the cold air had frozen the milk in the pail! Imagine how cold it was if the milk froze in minutes.

The temperature, in part, determines how quickly something freezes. Your kitchen freezer should be about 0° F (–18° C). Pour a couple of inches of milk in a container and place it in the freezer. Check on your milk every 20 minutes. How long does it take to freeze? Enjoy a nice milk slushy after your experiment.

Shop for Dishes

Manly and Laura looked in the Montgomery Ward catalog for their first Christmas gift. Together, they chose a set of glass dishes as their gift to one another.

Visit the website of Montgomery Ward or another department store and pick out your favorite dish pattern. How much would it cost to get all the dishes you want?

A Long Short Walk

A dust storm kept Peter and the sheep away for too long, so Manly went to help. It took them over an hour to walk just 400 yards (370 m) back to the barn because the wind repeatedly blew the sheep over.

Challenge yourself to walk slowly for 400 yards (370 m), which is about a quarter mile (0.4 km). How long did it take? Can you go slower? What if you pause between each step like the wind is stopping you? Play the role of the sheep and pretend the wind knocks you to the ground occasionally—then try to get up without using your hands. Have a friend blindfold you and guide you the distance. What was the longest amount of time it took you to walk the distance with the challenges?

Emergency Planning

During the cyclone, Laura and Rose went to the cellar. Laura also knew to escape the fire with Rose when it couldn't be put out with water.

Talk with your family. Create plans together of what to do in case of emergencies in your home.

Tornado Safety: Go to the lowest level of your home, like a basement or cellar. In a home without a basement or cellar, avoid windows. Lay face down in an interior room, hallway, or under a stairwell.

Fire Safety: Plan a family meeting spot that is away from your home. It might be your mailbox, a tree, or a neighbor's driveway. The goal is to exit your home as quickly as possible. Ask your family to have a practice fire drill.

HOUSE TALK

- If you have read the other Little House books, do you think Laura really minded the hard work of farming? How do you think she felt about farmers not having a lot of money?
- Laura was a pioneer girl as a child. Do you think she was also a farmer when she lived with her parents?
- Manly invested a lot of money in his tools and equipment. Mr. Larsen borrowed tools and didn't return them. It upset Laura. Manly wanted to be neighborly.

Laura disliked how Mr. Larsen took advantage of Manly. Is it better to be neighborly and lose your tools or to not lend them in the first place?

- Laura was in the house when some American Indians were on the property. What upset Laura while she was inside her house? Why did Laura go to the barn where the American Indians were if she was afraid?
- One of the American Indian visitors wanted Laura to go away with him to be his wife. What characteristic do you think he saw in Laura that he liked?
- Just as Laura expected, Manly and Laura had a baby girl. Do you remember why Laura chose the name Rose?
- Manly worked before he fully recovered from diphtheria. What do you know about Manly that explains why he did this?
- With another failed crop, do you think Manly was a bad farmer? Do you think the fourth year of farming was successful?
- Laura's childhood prepared her to not live in fear of wolves. Was it foolish or wise of her to check on the sheep?

10

What Happened Next

LEAVING DE SMET

Laura and Almanzo Wilder needed to recover from their losses on the farm, and Almanzo needed to improve his health, so they moved. Almanzo, Laura, and Rose lived briefly in Minnesota and then Florida. They returned to De Smet in 1892. Both Almanzo and Laura worked odd jobs to earn money.

In 1894—when Rose was just 7 years old—the family loaded a horse-drawn hack (carriage) and moved again. This time they went to Mansfield, Missouri. With a $100 bill as a down payment, they bought 40 acres of land with a small cabin. They named it Rocky Ridge Farm.

At first they lived by clearing the land and selling the timber. Laura sold eggs from her brown leghorn hens. Almanzo worked as a delivery man. Eventually, Laura designed her dream home, and Almanzo built it. Laura and Almanzo farmed Rocky Ridge together.

Rose eventually grew up and married Claire Gillette Lane, though the two later divorced. Rose Wilder Lane became a well-known novelist and writer. She encouraged Laura to write too.

THE INGALLS FAMILY

After Almanzo and Laura moved away from De Smet, they stayed in touch with their families through letters. They even returned to South Dakota to visit.

Charles and Caroline Ingalls left their homestead. Charles built a house on Third Street in De Smet, and the Ingalls moved to town for good. They were active citizens in their community. Charles worked mostly as a carpenter. He died in

Laura Ingalls Wilder in 1894, age 27, wearing her black wedding dress. *South Dakota State Historical Society*

1902. After his death, Caroline rented rooms to boarders to earn money. Caroline died in 1924.

In 1889, Mary Ingalls graduated from the Iowa School for the Blind. She became the first family member to graduate from college. Mary lived with her parents in De Smet. She helped with household chores and earned money selling her crafts. Grace and her husband lived with Mary after Caroline died. After suffering a stroke, Mary died in 1928.

Carrie Ingalls (whose real name was Caroline, like her mother), worked as an apprentice at the local newspaper after high school. She learned typesetting and printing at the *De Smet Leader*. She traveled and homesteaded before marrying David Swanzey in 1912. Carrie was stepmother to David's children, though she didn't have any children of her own. They lived in Keystone, South Dakota. Carrie Swanzey died in 1946.

After graduating from high school, Grace Ingalls took teacher's courses at Redfield College. Afterward, she taught several terms as a schoolteacher. She married a

The Ingalls Family in 1894. From the left: Caroline, Carrie, Laura, Charles, Grace, and Mary.
South Dakota State Historical Society

farmer named Nate Dow in 1901. They lived on Nate's family farm in Manchester, South Dakota, which was about 11 miles (18 km) from De Smet. Grace Dow died in 1941.

THE WRITING LIFE

Laura began writing for the *Missouri Ruralist* in 1911. It was (and is) a newspaper for farmers. Her popular column gave advice on life and farming. Laura wrote for the *Ruralist* until 1924. Other publications also featured Laura's writing, including a national magazine named *McCall's*.

Around 1930, Laura realized she had lived through a time in American history that few people had experienced or understood. Now in her sixties, she wanted to tell her childhood story.

Laura bought a few cheap notebooks and pencils. She began to write. This time, she didn't write a newspaper column. She wrote about her life. She focused

Laura Ingalls Wilder and Rose Wilder Lane. *South Dakota State Historical Society*

on her family's pioneer experience. She wrote until she filled six tablets with her story. She called her memoir *Pioneer Girl*.

Rose edited Laura's writing and sent it to publishers. The Great Depression changed the economy. No publisher wanted *that* book. But one editor liked the idea of Laura's story if it could be written as a children's novel.

Laura set to work. She included the real people and places of her childhood. But she fictionalized some parts of her writing. Some changes improved the story. Other times she left out parts that didn't fit in with the book family's characteristics of hard work and independence.

Rose continued to act as an editor for Laura. She suggested revisions—and sometimes just made the changes for her mother. Rose even submitted the manuscript to get published.

In 1932 Harper & Brothers (now called HarperCollins) published *Little House in the Big Woods*. Children loved it! It was an instant success.

Laura was already at work on her next book. *Farmer Boy* also focused on hard work and family life. It told the story of Almanzo Wilder's childhood in New York State.

She was just getting started. During Laura Ingalls Wilder's life, eight Little House books were published. Five of them were named as Newbery Honor Books, which is a special award in children's literature. A ninth book called *The First Four Years* was published after her death.

Rose traveled the world as a writer, but she often returned to Rocky Ridge Farm. Sometimes she would visit. Other times she lived there.

Almanzo and Laura lived comfortably, though modestly, in Mansfield. In 1949,

Laura Ingalls Wilder, age 70. *Photo © Laura Ingalls Wilder Home & Museum, Mansfield, Missouri*

Rocky Ridge Farm in Mansfield, Missouri, was home to Laura and Almanzo Wilder for 63 years and is open to visitors today. *Photo © Laura Ingalls Wilder Home & Museum, Mansfield, Missouri*

Almanzo died. Laura lived another ten years. She died just three days after her 90th birthday on February 10, 1957. She was buried beside Almanzo in Mansfield, Missouri.

Today readers around the world celebrate Laura Ingalls Wilder and read her Little House books.

This was the last home built by Charles Ingalls for his family. It's on Third Street in De Smet, South Dakota, and open to visitors. *Photo © Laura Ingalls Wilder Memorial Society, De Smet, South Dakota*

GLOSSARY OF PIONEER TERMS

Throughout the Little House series, you may encounter words that you've never heard before—or perhaps words used in ways we no longer use them today. Here's a guide to many of the unique terms that Laura Ingalls Wilder used in her books.

A

accordion: a portable musical instrument that you play by squeezing while pressing keys and buttons
anvil: a heavy metal block where blacksmiths shape tools and other metalworking
auger: a tool used to drill holes
awl: a pointed tool used to make holes, often in leather

B

baching: living as a bachelor or unmarried man
banknotes: a type of note made by a bank, which promises the owner money
basin: a large, round container that is wider than it is deep
basque: part of a woman's dress between the shoulders and waist
baste: to sew together loosely and temporarily
batten: thin strips of wood used to seal or reinforce a joint
bay pony: a reddish-brown pony with black mane, tail, and lower legs
beau: boyfriend
bed shoes: slippers
bedstead: bed frame

beholden: indebted, or owing something
belfry: a bell tower
bellow: a hand-pumped device that blows air into a forge to make sure the flame stays hot enough for metalworking
betroth: to promise to marry
binder: machine that cuts and fastens small grains, such as wheat, together in bunches
birk: a birch tree
bit: part of the bridle that goes in the horse's mouth
blouse: a shirt
blue stem: a type of grass
bluffs: a steep bank or cliff
bluing bag: a material used to brighten and whiten fabric that turned yellow from soap and age
board-bill: the expenses of renting a room
boarders: renters
boarding shanty: a place to pay for meals and a resting place
bobolink: a songbird
bodice: the upper part of a woman's dress
bole: tree trunk
bombazine: a silk and twilled fabric
bootjack: a device used to pull off boots or shoes
bore: to make a hole by drilling
bosom: chest
bough: tree branch
braid: hair or other material divided into three sections and woven together
braille: a writing system that uses raised dots to represent letters
braille slate: a board to help blind people write using braille
briar: prickly or thorny plant
brindle: gray or brown with streaks or spots
brine: a salt and water mixture for seasoning meat
brooch: a large pin worn near the neck
buckshot: small, round lead pellets used as a gun's ammunition
buckskin gelding: a castrated horse the color of a deer

buffalo wallows: a shallow dip in the prairie land that held water for bison to drink
buggy: a light carriage pulled by a horse
bulrush: a tall plant that grows near water
bushel: a unit of measure equal to 32 quarts, about the size of a laundry basket
buttonhook: a hook used to take a small button through a buttonhole

C

cakes: cookie-like desserts
caldron: a kettle for cooking over a fire
calico: fabric with small print or design
cambric: a thin, white fabric
capstan: a machine for moving heavy loads
cartridge: a container that holds bullets or pellets for a gun
cash crop: a plant grown to sell for profit
cashmere: wool made from goat hair
ceil: to furnish with a ceiling or lining
cellar: a room or space under a house that is often used for storage
chaff: the unusable seed covering on grain
challis: lightweight, soft fabric used for clothing
chilblain: swelling and sores due to exposure to extreme cold
chink: to fill in cracks or slits
chinook (Chinook): a warm wind
chirk: to cheer someone up
churn: the container used to make butter or the act of making butter from cream
cipher: to do math
claim shanty: a small cabin built quickly to show ownership of land
coal hod: a metal pail for carrying coal
cobbler: a person who makes and repairs shoes
cockerel: a young male chicken
coffee mill: a tool used to grind coffee beans
colander: a bowl-shaped utensil used to wash and drain liquid from foods
colt: a young horse or donkey
consumption: a disease also known as tuberculosis that affects the lungs

copper plate: very neat handwriting similar to the careful lettering used in engravings
cord: a pile of cut wood typically about 4 feet wide, 4 feet high, and 8 feet long
corncrib: a ventilated structure used to store dried corn
corset: an undergarment for women
coulter: a cutting tool attached to a plow
coverlet: bedspread
cracklings: bits of fried pork skin or fat
cravat: necktie or scarf
crinoline: a full, stiff undergarment worn under a dress or skirt
crochet: to make cloth from yarn or thread using hooked needles
cud: food regurgitated by animals like cows
cupola: a small structure on top of a building often used for ventilation
curd: solid cheese made when milk thickens
curl-paper: a strip of paper used to make hair curly
curry comb: a comb for horses
cutter: a lightweight sleigh

D

damper: a device that changes or stops the flow of air in a stove
dasher: long mixer used with a churn to make butter
deer-lick: a salty spot on the ground where deer come to lick salt
delaine: a high-quality wool fabric
denim: a sturdy fabric used for jeans, coats, and overalls
deportment: manners and behavior
depot: train station
doe: an adult female deer
doily: a mat often made of lace for decoration
down: soft, fluffy feathers
draught (draft): a device used to move air
dropleaf table: a table with sides that fold down
dry goods: fabrics and ready-to-buy clothing
dugout: a shelter or home built into a hillside
dust devil: a whirlwind made of sand or dirt

E

embroidery: pictures made from thread on fabric
emigrant car: freight car of a train with benches added temporarily for passengers
equinoctial storm: a violent storm near the first day of spring or fall
ewe: female sheep

F

false front: the front of a building that is taller than the roof
fanning mill: a tool that removed dirt, straw, and weeds from grains like wheat and oats
fascinator: a type of headpiece worn as a hat alternative
fawn: a young deer identified by the white spots on its back
fever 'n' ague: an illness called malaria
fichu-lace: a triangular scarf made of lace and draped around a woman's shoulders
fife: a small flute-like instrument
firebreak: plowed land intended to stop a fire from spreading
flank: a cut of meat
flannel: a soft fabric made from cotton or wool
flatiron (flat iron): a tool made from iron used to press and remove wrinkles from clothing
fleece: coat of wool from an animal like a sheep
flying shuttle: a device used to make weaving quicker
ford: a shallow area of a river or creek making it easier to cross
forenoon: morning or the time before noon
freshet: a stream's flood caused by heavy rains or melting snow
frier: a chicken between 6 and 8 weeks old
frock: a man's outer shirt worn for work or a woman's dress
furrow: a trench or ditch made by a plow

G

gaiters: a covering of cloth or leather worn as a shoe or over a shoe
galluses: suspenders
game: wild animals that are hunted for food or sport

geezer: an odd, elderly man
gild: to cover with a thin layer of gold
gilt: golden color
gored skirt: a skirt made from triangular pieces
grainery (granary): a structure used to store grain
grippe: a contagious disease, today called influenza
grist mill: a mill for grinding grain such as flour
grubbing hoe: a long gardening tool used to dig up vegetables that grow underground, such as potatoes
gulch: a deep ravine
gully: a narrow ditch
gunny sack: a bag made from burlap

H

hair receiver: a container to collect loose hair from a woman's comb
hair-switch: a loose hair extension used to style or fill out the top or sides of hair
hand cradle: a hand tool used to gather stalks of grain, such as oats or wheat
handcar: a railroad car powered by people
handsled: a small sled pulled by hand
hardtack: a hard biscuit or cracker made without salt
harness: a set of leather straps connecting a horse to a wagon or cart
harrow: to break up soil
hassock: a low stool or padded cushion
hasty pudding: a porridge made from ground corn or oatmeal
hatchet: a small ax
headcheese: slow-cooked pork formed into a loaf
hearth: the floor in front of a fireplace
heifer: a young female cow that has not had her first calf
hewed: to cut with heavy blows
hickory bow: curved, flexible piece of hickory wood
hide: the skin of an animal
hitching post: a vertical post where animals such as horses can be tied
hoarfrost: frost
hoarhound candy: a hard, bittersweet candy

hodful: the amount of coal that can be carried in a metal pail
hogshead: a large container to store liquid
hoopskirt: an undergarment worn by women to add fullness to a dress or skirt
hornpipe: a musical instrument made from a wooden or bone pipe
hulled corn: cooked and softened corn kernels without their skins

I

Indian summer: an old term for warm weather in late fall; the origin of the phrase is debated, but it's possible that settlers used the term because of harmful stereotypes about American Indians, so it's best not to use it today
isinglass: clear, white, or semi-transparent material

J

jabot: decorative clothing accessory made of lace worn near the throat
jack-knife (jackknife): a pocket knife with a foldable blade
jamboree: a large, often noisy, gathering
jew's harp: a small instrument placed against the teeth or lips; known today as a mouth harp or jaw harp
jig: a type of energetic folk dance, typically including rapid movement of the feet
jumper: overalls

K

keg: a small barrel
kerosene: a type of fuel used to produce heat, light, or power
kilted: tucked up
knoll: a small hill

L

laddie: a boy
lard: solid fat, often from pork
lass: a girl
last: the molded shape of a foot used in shoe making and repair
latchstring: a string on a latch that opens and locks a door
lath: narrow strips of wood

lawn: lightweight fabric often made from cotton
lean-to: a small shack or shed built onto a house with a sloped roof
leech: a bloodsucking worm
lick and a promise: a careless or hasty job
livery barn: a stable where horses are kept in the community
looking glass: mirror
lope: a quick movement, typically by an animal such as a horse or rabbit
lye: a strong chemical used for cleaning
lynch pin (linchpin): a small pin to hold items together

M

mad dog: a sick dog infected with rabies
manger: an open box in a barn or stable for animal food
manure: solid waste from farm animals
mare: a female horse
meal: cornmeal
merchant: a seller such as a store owner
merino: a soft, high-quality wool
milch cow: a cow used for its milk
minstrel: a musical entertainer
missionary: a member of a religious group serving others
moccasin: a soft leather shoe
Morgan: a breed of light, strong horses
mosquito bar: a net used as a screen to protect against mosquitoes and other small insects
mother-of-pearl: the shiny inner coating on some seashells
muff: a scarf
muffler: a scarf
muslin: a thin cotton fabric
mustang: a small wild horse

N

naught: nothing
nigh: close or near

no'm: slang for "no, ma'am"
noose: a rope with a slipknot
nubbin: a small object

O

Old Glory: a nickname for the US flag
orthography: the art of writing words or the study of language
Osage: a nation of American Indians
ought (aught): zero
ox goad: a long stick used to guide cattle

P

padlock: a removable lock
pannikin: a small pan
papoose: a word for *baby* taken from the Narragansett language that many settlers came to use to describe all American Indian babies; because of the generalization, the term is typically seen as offensive today
parasol: a lightweight umbrella intended to provide shade from the sun
parlor: a room used to entertain guests
pasteboard: cardboard
petticoat: a long, loose undergarment worn under a dress
picket line: a rope attached to a horse and anchored to a tree or the ground
pigeon hole: a small compartment, often in a desk
pink: to cut with a saw-tooth edge
plait: braid
plank: a thick board
plate: an illustration showing a fashion trend
plough (plow): to turn over soil to prepare it for seed
plum thicket: a group of plum trees
plumb line: a tool used to determine if something is vertical
pocketbook: a wallet or purse
poke bonnet: a women's bonnet with a wide front brim
polka: a lively dance
poplin: a strong fabric

porthole: an opening or a window
posy: a flower
poultice: a mixture of materials such as herbs used as medicine on the skin
powder-horn: a container for gunpowder, often made from a cow or ox's horn
prairie: level land covered in grass with few trees
pre-emption (preemption): allowing one person to make a purchase before offering it to others
provisions: needed materials or supplies
pullet: a young hen
pumphouse (pump house): a small building that houses water equipment, like a water pump or well
puncheon floor: floorboards made from split logs

Q

quicksand: wet sand you can sink into
quinine: a type of medication used to treat malaria

R

ramrod: a long, slender pole used to clean the inside of a gun barrel
reaper: farm machinery that cuts grain
receipt: recipe
recitation: the act of speaking publicly from memory
reel: a device that is used to wind something
rein: a leather strap attached to a horse's bridle used to control the horse
revolver: a handgun
rheumatism: pain and stiffness of the back
rick: a stack of hay, straw, or corn in a field
robes: blankets made of fabric or animal hides
roller towel: a towel with its ends sewn together and hung over a bar
rosin: to cover with varnish or resin
rush: a marsh plant

S

sadiron: a flat iron with pointed ends and a handle
saleratus: baking soda

saloon: a public bar
salt-pork: a meat like bacon but saltier and cut into large slabs
satchel: a small bag
savage: a term historically used to refer to someone considered to be less civilized or part of a wild society, now considered very offensive
scalawag: a southern white person who supported government reconstruction after the Civil War; a young person who causes trouble
scalp: to remove the scalp from the head
scalp-lock (scalp lock): pieces of hair on a shaved head
scarlet fever: a contagious illness with symptoms including a red rash, sore throat, and high fever
scholar: student
scrabble: to scratch or claw wildly
scythe: a long-handled tool with a blade used for cutting grass and grains
seed wheat: wheat seeds intended for planting
shanty: a small cabin
shawl: a piece of clothing worn by women around the shoulders and often shaped like a triangle
sheaf: a bundle of grain
shears: scissors
sheep sorrel: a plant in the buckwheat family
sheepfold: a pen for sheep
shingle: a building material used in overlapping rows such as on a roof
shirr: to gather cloth on a thread
shock: a group of bundles of grain
shot: a small ball of lead used in a gun's bullet
sieve: a mesh utensil used to separate liquids and solids
silk: a fine-quality fabric made from the thread of silkworms
skein: a loosely coiled section of yarn
skid: planks used to lift an object
slate: small blackboard used as a writing surface
slough: a swamp or marsh area
snow blind: eye swelling and light sensitivity due to the sun's reflection on snow
sod: the top layer of soil where grass grows
soda: baking soda

sorrel: orangish-brown
sow: to plant seeds
spade: a small tool used for digging
sprigged: marked with pictures of plants
squaw: a term with unknown origins—possibly a corruption of terms in some Eastern Algonquian languages—that white pioneers often used for American Indian women or wives; now considered very offensive
stable: a barn
stall: a compartment in a barn for an animal
stanchion: a device around an animal's neck that limits movement
starch: to stiffen
Stars and Stripes: a nickname for the US flag
steer: a young male bovine, such as a cow or ox
stock: farm animals
stockade: an enclosed area to protect against attacks
stockings: socks, usually knit
straw-tick: mattress made of cloth and filled with straw or other plant material
studding: the boards providing the frame of a room or building
surveyor: someone whose job it is to collect information about an area of land
swathes: a row of cut grass or grain
switch: a bundle of hair used with a person's natural hair; or, a slender whip

T

tableland: a large area of level land with a cliff or sharp edge on one side
tallow: fat from cattle and sheep used in candle making and soap making
tar-paper (tar paper): a heavy paper coated in tar used in construction
thicket: a thick group of trees or shrubs
thimble: a small, protective covering for a fingertip used during sewing
thong: a narrow strip of leather
thoroughbred: bred for many generations from a reputable breed of animals
thresh: to separate the part of the grain you can eat from the other parts
tick: the shell of a mattress or pillow made from fabric
till: a box, drawer, or tray
timber: cut wood used for building materials

tintype: a type of photography
train: the long back part of a gown that trails behind the wearer
treadle: a foot lever that powers a machine
treaty: an agreement made by talking and negotiation
trough: a box-like container that holds food or water for animals
trousers: pants
trundle bed: a small bed stored under a larger bed when not in use
tuft: a group of items held tightly together at the bottom but loose at the top

U

udder: a bag-like milk-producing organ on a cow
Uncle Sam: a nickname for the US government
union suit: a one-piece undergarment

V

valise: suitcase
velocipede: a bicycle or tricycle
venison: deer meat

W

waist: a shirt
warpath: a route used by American Indians to go to war
wash basin: a bowl for water usually used for washing the hands and face
washboard: a bumpy tool for washing clothes
wash-boiler (washboiler): a large metal container used to boil and clean clothing
weevil: a type of beetle
whalebones: bone from a whale used to stiffen a woman's undergarments
what-not (whatnot): a piece of furniture with open shelves
whetstone: a stone used to sharpen knives and tools
whey: the liquid formed when milk is made into cheese
whiffletree: a crossbar attached to something a horse is pulling
whip: to make a temporary seam or hem
whiskey: a type of liquor

whitewash: an inexpensive paint made from lime
whittle: to cut or carve with a knife
windlass: a machine using a crank and rope to lift items
windrow: a row of hay or other grain ready to be baled or stored
winnow: to separate chaff from usable grain
withe: a slender branch
worsted yarn: a smooth type of yarn
writ of attachment: a court order directing a member of law enforcement to take property from a defendant

Y

yearling: an animal that is one year old
yoke: a bar attached to the neck of two animals or to the shoulders of a person
young cuss: slang for a young man

RESOURCES TO EXPLORE

PLACES TO VISIT

Laura Ingalls Wilder lived in many "little houses" throughout her life. Many of the places she wrote about are now museums you can visit. If you can't go in person, consider using Google Earth or another online program to take a virtual tour.

Laura Ingalls Wilder Museum
306 3rd Street (Hwy 35), PO Box 269
Pepin, Wisconsin 54759
715-513-6383
www.lauraingallspepin.com

Little House Wayside Cabin
N3228 Cty CC
Stockholm, Wisconsin 54769
The Laura Ingalls Wilder Memorial Society operates a museum and gift shop in the village of Pepin and hosts Laura Days annually in September (www.lauradays.org). The society also maintains the Little House Wayside Cabin, which is built on three acres of land that were part of Charles and Caroline Ingalls's farm, the birthplace of Laura Ingalls Wilder. The cabin is just 7 miles (11 km) north of Pepin and is open every day of the year for visitors (but has no water or electricity).

Little House on the Prairie Museum
Little House on the Prairie Museum
2507 CR 3000
Independence, Kansas 67301
620-289-4238
www.littlehouseontheprairiemuseum.com

The Little House on the Prairie Museum educates the public about Laura Ingalls Wilder and her books in addition to life on the prairie in the late 1800s and early 1900s. The museum is on the original land where the Ingalls family lived in 1870.

Laura Ingalls Wilder Museum

330 Eighth Street
Walnut Grove, Minnesota 56180
800-528-7280 or 507-859-2358
www.walnutgrove.org
The Laura Ingalls Wilder Museum has several buildings for visitors to learn the history of Laura Ingalls Wilder and Walnut Grove. Visit a dugout the same size as the one the Ingalls family lived in and a replica pioneer house like the one Pa built in *On the Banks of Plum Creek*. Enjoy an outdoor theater production of Laura's life in Walnut Grove three weekends every July.

Laura Ingalls Wilder Park & Museum

3603 236th Avenue
Burr Oak, Iowa 52101
563-735-5916
www.lauraingallswilder.us
The Masters Hotel, now the Laura Ingalls Wilder Park & Museum, is in Burr Oak, Iowa. This is where the Ingalls family lived and worked from 1876 to 1877. It's also the birthplace of Grace Ingalls. Guided tours are offered at the Masters Hotel, the only childhood home of Laura Ingalls Wilder that remains standing on its original site.

Ingalls Homestead

20812 Homestead Road
De Smet, South Dakota 57231
605-854-3984
www.ingallshomestead.com
The Ingalls Homestead is located on the land Charles Ingalls earned from the Homestead Act and turned into a farm. Visitors experience pioneer heritage through hands-on activities. Drive a covered wagon, attend a one-room schoolhouse, make ropes and corn cob dolls, twist haysticks and grind wheat, and camp on the open prairie like Laura described in her books.

Laura Ingalls Wilder Memorial Society

105 Olivet Avenue
De Smet, South Dakota 57231
800-880-3383
www.discoverlaura.org

Discover Laura while visiting the Surveyors' House, the First School of De Smet, Pa's homestead, and the final home of Charles and Caroline Ingalls. The Discover Center hosts pioneer activities and the museum contains original Ingalls Wilder items.

The Laura Ingalls Wilder Historic Home and Museum

3060 Highway A
Mansfield, Missouri 65704
877-924-7126
www.lauraingallswilderhome.com

The Laura Ingalls Wilder Historic Home and Museum in Mansfield, Missouri, was home to Laura and Almanzo for 63 years. The Wilders spent 17 years building their farmhouse, where the Little House series would eventually be written. The home stands today just as Laura left it in February 1957.

The Almanzo Wilder Homestead

177 Stacy Road
Malone, New York 12953
518-483-1207
www.almanzowilderfarm.com

The Almanzo & Laura Ingalls Wilder Association (ALIWA) maintains the Almanzo Wilder Homestead in Burke, New York: the original home of Almanzo Wilder and site of *Farmer Boy*. The 84-acre homestead includes a restored farmhouse (1840–1843), reconstructed barns and outbuildings, a replica one-room schoolhouse, and more. The visitor center includes a museum, a research library, archives, and a gift shop.

Spring Valley Methodist Church Museum

221 West Courtland Street
Spring Valley, Minnesota 55975
507-346-7659
www.springvalleymnmuseum.org

The Wilder family lived in Spring Valley for more than thirty years. The Wilders attended church in the Methodist church building. A section of the Spring Valley Methodist Church Museum is dedicated to the family of Almanzo Wilder. Additional museum displays include historical information about Spring Valley and the Methodist church.

BOOKS, WEBSITES, AND VIDEOS

Find out more about Laura Ingalls Wilder's fascinating life.

A few books about Laura Ingalls Wilder for children or adults:

Laura Ingalls Wilder: A Biography, by William Anderson
Laura Ingalls Wilder Country, by William Anderson
Laura's Album: A Remembrance Scrapbook of Laura Ingalls Wilder, by William Anderson
The Little House Cookbook, by Barbara M. Walker
The Little House Guidebook, by William Anderson
A Little House Traveler, by Laura Ingalls Wilder
Prairie Girl, by William Anderson
The World of Little House, by Carolyn Strom Collins and Christina Wyss Eriksson

A few books about Laura Ingalls Wilder for adults:

Becoming Laura Ingalls Wilder, by John E. Miller
Laura Ingalls Wilder and Education in Kingsbury County, Dakota Territory 1880–1885, by Nancy S. Cleaveland
Laura Ingalls Wilder: A Writer's Life, by Pamela Smith Hill
Laura Ingalls Wilder, Farm Journalist, edited by Stephen W. Hines
Laura Ingalls Wilder's Little Town, by John E. Miller
Little House Traveler, by Laura Ingalls Wilder
Pioneer Girl, by Laura Ingalls Wilder annotated by Pamela Smith Hill
Pioneer Girl Perspectives, edited by Nancy Tystad Koupal
A Prairie Girl's Faith, by Stephen W. Hines
Prairie Fires, by Caroline Fraser
The World of Laura Ingalls Wilder, by Marta McDowell

Websites to Visit

These are just a few sites to explore to learn more about the life of Laura Ingalls Wilder.

www.beyondlittlehouse.com
www.discoverlaura.wordpress.com
www.faithofliw.wordpress.com
www.hoover.archives.gov/education/rose-wilder-lane-and-laura-ingalls-wilder
www.littlehousebooks.com
www.littlehouseontheprairie.com
www.liwfrontiergirl.com
www.pioneergirl.com
www.pioneergirlproject.org
www.trundlebedtales.com
www.wildercompanion.com

Films and Videos

Almanzo Wilder: Life Before Laura, Legacy Documentaries, 2012.
Little House on the Prairie: The Legacy of Laura Ingalls Wilder, Legacy Documentaries, 2014.

ACTIVITIES LIST

Activities and Games

- Snow Pictures
- The Quiet Challenge
- Visit a Maple Farm
- Dance a Jig
- Rag Curls
- Stump Jump
- Giddap!
- Grass Whistle
- Visit Malone's Square
- Cracked Ice
- Fire Starter
- Outdoor Laundry
- Living Light Test
- Hide the Thimble
- Cat's Cradle
- Sweet Potato Garden
- Feed a Grasshopper
- Grow Grass
- See for Mary
- Night Hike
- Clothesline Path
- Declaration!
- Charades
- Drop the Handkerchief
- Pack Up!
- Countdown
- Writing Challenge
- House Count Challenge
- Three Blind Mice in Rounds
- Grow a Geranium
- Shop for Dishes
- A Long Short Walk
- Emergency Planning

Crafts

- Paper Dolls
- Clove-Apple
- Tin Lantern
- Alice's Air-Castle
- Log House Craft
- Star Garland
- Popcorn String
- Homemade Checker Board
- Braided Rag Trivet
- Name Cards
- Beaded Bracelet

Food and Recipes

- Homemade Butter
- Vinegar Pie
- Pancake People
- Snow Maple Candy
- Nut Taste Test
- Johnnycakes
- Strawberry Jam
- Popcorn and Milk Challenge
- Apples 'n' Onions
- Self-Turning Old-Fashioned Doughnuts
- Pink Lemonade
- Homemade Ice Cream
- Dried Berries
- Corn Dodgers with Molasses
- Dumplings and Gravy
- Stewed Plums
- Vanity Cakes
- Dried Apples
- Soda Crackers
- Sour-Milk Biscuits
- Hot Biscuits with Honey or Applesauce
- Sage and Onion Stuffing
- Ginger Water
- Cambric Tea
- Buckwheat Pancakes
- Cranberry Jelly
- Chicken Pie with Biscuit Crust
- Popcorn Balls
- Corn Bread
- Pieplant Pie
- Homemade Bread

ACKNOWLEDGMENTS

I'm so grateful for my husband, Derek, who supports my writing passion. Our children, Meghan, Evan, and Esther, gave me the inspiration to write this book and tested countless activities and recipes with me.

Thank you to my family and friends who believed in this book . . . and me. My sister, Amy, cheers the loudest. It means the world to me.

A special thank you to my beta readers and writing partners, especially Sara Matson and Tracy Vonder Brink. This book is better because of you.

Thank you, Lisa Reardon, for believing in this project, and Jerome Pohlen, for seeing it through at Chicago Review Press.

I thank Bill Anderson, Nancy Cleaveland, and Jim and Marilyn Lusk for their expertise and conversations about this manuscript. Thank you to all the Laura Ingalls Wilder experts who share their passion and knowledge with curious readers.

This book wouldn't be in your hands without the inspiring books of Laura Ingalls Wilder. Her books have taught countless readers about life on the American prairie. She lives on through the home sites. I thank the museums for preserving Wilder's legacy for passionate and curious fans. I appreciate the conversations I had with various helpful and knowledgeable staff and volunteers.

And I'm grateful to God who prepared me for this project when I wasn't looking.

HEADING WEST

LIFE WITH THE PIONEERS, 21 ACTIVITIES

PAT MCCARTHY

978-1-55652-809-5 • $16.95 (CAN $18.95) • Also available in ebook formats.

Tracing the vivid saga of Native American and pioneer men, women, and children, *Heading West* covers the colonial beginnings of the westward expansion to the last of the homesteaders in the late 20th century. More than 20 activities are included in this engaging guide to life in the west, including learning to churn butter, making dip candles, tracking animals, playing Blind Man's Bluff, and creating a homestead diorama.